SPECTRUM®

Multiplication

Grade 3

Spectrum®
An imprint of Carson-Dellosa Publishing LLC
P.O. Box 35665
Greensboro, NC 27425 USA

ISBN 978-1-4838-0474-3

04-292151151

Table of Contents Grade 3

Spectrum Multiplication is designed to build a solid foundation in multiplication for your third grader. Aligned to the third grade Common Core State Standards for multiplication, every page equips your child with the confidence to master multiplication. Helpful examples provide step-by-step guidance to teach new concepts, followed by a variety of practice pages that will sharpen your child's skills and efficiency at problem solving. Use the Pretests, Posttests, Mid-Test, and Final Test as the perfect way to track your child's progress and identify where he or she needs extra practice.

Common Core State Standards Alignment: Multiplication Grade 3

Domain: Operations and Algebraic Thinking	
Standard	Aligned Practice Pages
3.OA.1	6–7, 32–33
3.OA.3	32–40, 43, 68–77, 81–82
3.OA.4	5–31, 41–42, 44–67, 78–80
3.OA.5	29–30, 39
3.OA.7	5–82
3.OA.8	32, 35, 38, 40, 43
3.OA.9	15, 19, 23, 27, 42, 79, 81
Domain: Number and Operations in Base Ten	
Standard	Aligned Practice Pages
3NBT.3	46–50, 56, 58–59, 62, 73, 78–81

NAME _____

 Check What You Know

Single Digit Multiplication

Multiply.

	a	b	c	d	e
1.	2 ×0	5 ×1	4 ×3	0 ×2	5 ×6
2.	7 ×2	9 ×3	8 ×8	6 ×3	4 ×5
3.	6 ×6	3 ×9	1 ×7	5 ×3	2 ×6
4.	3 ×0	4 ×7	6 ×9	4 ×4	5 ×1
5.	7 ×4	3 ×7	2 ×3	4 ×2	9 ×1

Fill in the missing number.

6.
□
× 8
——
24

5
× □
——
20

2
× □
——
4

□
× 9
——
18

6
× □
——
30

Understanding Multiplication

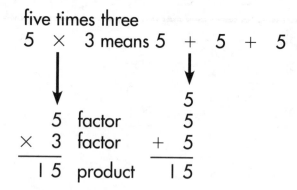

two times seven
2 × 7 means 7 + 7

7	factor	7
× 2	factor	+ 7
1 4	product	1 4

five times three
5 × 3 means 5 + 5 + 5

		5
5	factor	5
× 3	factor	+ 5
1 5	product	1 5

Multiply. Write the corresponding addition problem next to each multiplication problem.

     a   **b**   **c**

1.
   3   3
 ×2 +3
  — —
  6   6

   7
×2

   6
×2

2.
   2
×2

   1
×2

   5
×3

3.
   2
×3

   1
×3

   4
×3

4.
   4
×4

   1
×4

   5
×4

Understanding Multiplication

Multiply. Write the corresponding addition problem next to each multiplication problem.

	a	b	c
1.	$\begin{array}{r} 9 \\ \times 2 \\ \hline \end{array}$	$\begin{array}{r} 8 \\ \times 2 \\ \hline \end{array}$	$\begin{array}{r} 6 \\ \times 3 \\ \hline \end{array}$
2.	$\begin{array}{r} 3 \\ \times 3 \\ \hline \end{array}$	$\begin{array}{r} 7 \\ \times 3 \\ \hline \end{array}$	$\begin{array}{r} 2 \\ \times 4 \\ \hline \end{array}$
3.	$\begin{array}{r} 9 \\ \times 4 \\ \hline \end{array}$	$\begin{array}{r} 8 \\ \times 4 \\ \hline \end{array}$	$\begin{array}{r} 3 \\ \times 4 \\ \hline \end{array}$
4.	$\begin{array}{r} 4 \\ \times 2 \\ \hline \end{array}$	$\begin{array}{r} 5 \\ \times 2 \\ \hline \end{array}$	$\begin{array}{r} 8 \\ \times 3 \\ \hline \end{array}$

Multiplying through 5 × 9

Multiply.

	a	b	c	d	e
1.	5 ×0	3 ×9	6 ×5	1 ×4	5 ×1
2.	9 ×2	8 ×5	5 ×8	0 ×0	2 ×9
3.	4 ×6	7 ×3	6 ×1	7 ×2	3 ×5
4.	6 ×2	5 ×5	9 ×1	2 ×4	3 ×7

Multiplying through 5 × 9

Multiply.

	a	b	c	d	e
1.	0 ×9	3 ×6	7 ×5	5 ×6	3 ×2
2.	7 ×4	3 ×3	1 ×9	2 ×7	0 ×6
3.	6 ×3	3 ×4	4 ×1	7 ×0	4 ×2
4.	1 ×3	4 ×4	3 ×6	4 ×5	1 ×5

Multiplying through 9 × 9

Multiply.

	a	**b**	**c**	**d**	**e**
1.	3 ×9	7 ×6	5 ×4	7 ×9	8 ×6
2.	4 ×3	8 ×5	4 ×9	3 ×0	5 ×7
3.	5 ×1	4 ×6	8 ×2	6 ×8	4 ×0
4.	3 ×1	6 ×4	9 ×2	3 ×4	6 ×3

Multiplying through 9 × 9

Multiply.

	a	b	c	d	e
1.	$\begin{array}{r} 5 \\ \times 0 \\ \hline \end{array}$	$\begin{array}{r} 2 \\ \times 9 \\ \hline \end{array}$	$\begin{array}{r} 0 \\ \times 9 \\ \hline \end{array}$	$\begin{array}{r} 5 \\ \times 6 \\ \hline \end{array}$	$\begin{array}{r} 3 \\ \times 8 \\ \hline \end{array}$
2.	$\begin{array}{r} 3 \\ \times 6 \\ \hline \end{array}$	$\begin{array}{r} 7 \\ \times 6 \\ \hline \end{array}$	$\begin{array}{r} 9 \\ \times 9 \\ \hline \end{array}$	$\begin{array}{r} 8 \\ \times 4 \\ \hline \end{array}$	$\begin{array}{r} 5 \\ \times 3 \\ \hline \end{array}$
3.	$\begin{array}{r} 2 \\ \times 6 \\ \hline \end{array}$	$\begin{array}{r} 8 \\ \times 8 \\ \hline \end{array}$	$\begin{array}{r} 9 \\ \times 3 \\ \hline \end{array}$	$\begin{array}{r} 7 \\ \times 4 \\ \hline \end{array}$	$\begin{array}{r} 8 \\ \times 0 \\ \hline \end{array}$
4.	$\begin{array}{r} 7 \\ \times 7 \\ \hline \end{array}$	$\begin{array}{r} 3 \\ \times 7 \\ \hline \end{array}$	$\begin{array}{r} 8 \\ \times 9 \\ \hline \end{array}$	$\begin{array}{r} 5 \\ \times 5 \\ \hline \end{array}$	$\begin{array}{r} 9 \\ \times 1 \\ \hline \end{array}$

Single Digit Multiplication

Multiply.

	a	b	c	d	e
1.	3 ×3	8 ×7	2 ×9	7 ×5	9 ×4
2.	9 ×9	4 ×3	5 ×3	4 ×4	7 ×7
3.	8 ×5	6 ×4	8 ×2	9 ×7	4 ×8
4.	1 ×1	9 ×5	8 ×6	7 ×6	9 ×6

Single Digit Multiplication

Multiply.

	a	**b**	**c**	**d**	**e**
1.	6 ×6	7 ×1	9 ×0	9 ×3	2 ×2
2.	3 ×3	7 ×3	5 ×5	9 ×8	7 ×8
3.	3 ×7	7 ×4	6 ×3	7 ×0	4 ×9
4.	6 ×5	2 ×7	9 ×1	3 ×9	6 ×8

SCORE ⬭ **/ 20**

Single Digit Multiplication

Multiply.

	a	b	c	d	e
1.	7 ×2	2 ×9	2 ×5	6 ×2	5 ×2
2.	8 ×2	2 ×4	2 ×6	2 ×1	9 ×2
3.	2 ×2	2 ×3	4 ×2	2 ×8	1 ×2
4.	2 ×0	2 ×7	3 ×2	2 ×1	0 ×2

Single Digit Multiplication

Multiply.

	a	b	c	d	e
1.	5 ×3	9 ×3	3 ×7	5 ×3	3 ×3
2.	8 ×3	6 ×3	3 ×1	7 ×3	3 ×2
3.	3 ×5	3 ×4	3 ×9	3 ×5	0 ×3

Complete each table.

a
4. Rule: multiply by 3

In	Out
2	
4	
6	18
8	

b
Rule: multiply by 5

In	Out
5	25
3	
7	
9	

c
Rule: multiply by 7

In	Out
4	28
8	
9	
7	

Single Digit Multiplication

Fill in the missing number.

a	b	c	d	e

1.

a. 6 × ☐ = 54

b. ☐ × 6 = 42

c. 5 × ☐ = 25

d. ☐ × 5 = 5

e. 8 × ☐ = 72

2.

a. 4 × ☐ = 16

b. 2 × ☐ = 8

c. ☐ × 5 = 15

d. ☐ × 7 = 49

e. ☐ × 2 = 6

3.

a. ☐ × 7 = 56

b. 8 × ☐ = 24

c. ☐ × 3 = 24

d. 9 × ☐ = 63

e. ☐ × 6 = 30

4.

a. 3 × ☐ = 15

b. ☐ × 8 = 64

c. 4 × ☐ = 32

d. ☐ × 5 = 45

e. 1 × ☐ = 8

Single Digit Multiplication

Multiply.

	a	b	c	d	e
1.	6 ×4	9 ×4	4 ×7	5 ×4	4 ×4
2.	8 ×4	4 ×6	4 ×1	7 ×4	4 ×2
3.	4 ×1	3 ×4	4 ×9	4 ×5	0 ×4
4.	4 ×3	4 ×8	1 ×4	2 ×4	4 ×7

SCORE ◯ / 20

Single Digit Multiplication

Multiply.

	a	b	c	d	e
1.	$\begin{array}{r} 5 \\ \times 6 \\ \hline \end{array}$	$\begin{array}{r} 4 \\ \times 5 \\ \hline \end{array}$	$\begin{array}{r} 2 \\ \times 5 \\ \hline \end{array}$	$\begin{array}{r} 5 \\ \times 9 \\ \hline \end{array}$	$\begin{array}{r} 5 \\ \times 2 \\ \hline \end{array}$
2.	$\begin{array}{r} 1 \\ \times 5 \\ \hline \end{array}$	$\begin{array}{r} 6 \\ \times 5 \\ \hline \end{array}$	$\begin{array}{r} 7 \\ \times 5 \\ \hline \end{array}$	$\begin{array}{r} 5 \\ \times 5 \\ \hline \end{array}$	$\begin{array}{r} 5 \\ \times 1 \\ \hline \end{array}$
3.	$\begin{array}{r} 5 \\ \times 3 \\ \hline \end{array}$	$\begin{array}{r} 0 \\ \times 5 \\ \hline \end{array}$	$\begin{array}{r} 5 \\ \times 8 \\ \hline \end{array}$	$\begin{array}{r} 9 \\ \times 5 \\ \hline \end{array}$	$\begin{array}{r} 5 \\ \times 7 \\ \hline \end{array}$
4.	$\begin{array}{r} 8 \\ \times 5 \\ \hline \end{array}$	$\begin{array}{r} 5 \\ \times 1 \\ \hline \end{array}$	$\begin{array}{r} 0 \\ \times 5 \\ \hline 0 \end{array}$	$\begin{array}{r} 3 \\ \times 5 \\ \hline \end{array}$	$\begin{array}{r} 5 \\ \times 4 \\ \hline \end{array}$

Single Digit Multiplication

Multiply.

	a	b	c	d	e
1.	6 ×5	9 ×5	5 ×7	5 ×5	5 ×4
2.	8 ×5	5 ×6	5 ×1	7 ×5	5 ×2
3.	5 ×1	3 ×5	5 ×9	4 ×5	0 ×5

Complete each table.

	a	b	c
4.	Rule: multiply by 4	Rule: multiply by 2	Rule: multiply by 6

In	Out
5	
1	
8	32
7	

In	Out
9	
2	
6	
3	6

In	Out
8	
4	24
6	
1	

SCORE ◯ **/ 20**

Single Digit Multiplication

Multiply.

	a	b	c	d	e
1.	0 ×6	2 ×6	6 ×6	6 ×9	7 ×6
2.	1 ×6	9 ×6	6 ×1	6 ×4	6 ×1
3.	6 ×7	4 ×6	5 ×6	8 ×6	3 ×6
4.	6 ×0	6 ×3	1 ×6	6 ×2	6 ×5

Single Digit Multiplication

Fill in the missing number.

	a	b	c	d	e

1.

a)
$$\begin{array}{r} 9 \\ \times\ 2 \\ \hline \square \end{array}$$

b)
$$\begin{array}{r} \square \\ \times\ 4 \\ \hline 12 \end{array}$$

c)
$$\begin{array}{r} 8 \\ \times\ 5 \\ \hline \square \end{array}$$

d)
$$\begin{array}{r} 5 \\ \times\ \square \\ \hline 30 \end{array}$$

e)
$$\begin{array}{r} 6 \\ \times\ 8 \\ \hline \square \end{array}$$

2.

a)
$$\begin{array}{r} \square \\ \times\ 3 \\ \hline 21 \end{array}$$

b)
$$\begin{array}{r} 1 \\ \times\ 2 \\ \hline \square \end{array}$$

c)
$$\begin{array}{r} 7 \\ \times\ \square \\ \hline 35 \end{array}$$

d)
$$\begin{array}{r} 3 \\ \times\ 5 \\ \hline \square \end{array}$$

e)
$$\begin{array}{r} 8 \\ \times\ \square \\ \hline 16 \end{array}$$

3.

a)
$$\begin{array}{r} \square \\ \times\ 2 \\ \hline 12 \end{array}$$

b)
$$\begin{array}{r} 4 \\ \times\ 6 \\ \hline \square \end{array}$$

c)
$$\begin{array}{r} 7 \\ \times\ \square \\ \hline 28 \end{array}$$

d)
$$\begin{array}{r} 3 \\ \times\ \square \\ \hline 27 \end{array}$$

e)
$$\begin{array}{r} \square \\ \times\ 5 \\ \hline 5 \end{array}$$

4.

a)
$$\begin{array}{r} 4 \\ \times\ 4 \\ \hline \square \end{array}$$

b)
$$\begin{array}{r} 6 \\ \times\ 6 \\ \hline \square \end{array}$$

c)
$$\begin{array}{r} 6 \\ \times\ \square \\ \hline 6 \end{array}$$

d)
$$\begin{array}{r} \square \\ \times\ 3 \\ \hline 24 \end{array}$$

e)
$$\begin{array}{r} 5 \\ \times\ \square \\ \hline 25 \end{array}$$

SCORE ⬭ **/ 20**

Single Digit Multiplication

Multiply.

	a	b	c	d	e
1.	5 ×7	7 ×8	6 ×7	7 ×0	9 ×7
2.	7 ×7	7 ×1	7 ×4	7 ×2	2 ×7
3.	7 ×1	2 ×7	8 ×7	7 ×6	3 ×7
4.	0 ×7	7 ×5	4 ×7	1 ×7	7 ×9

SCORE ⬭ **/ 20**

Single Digit Multiplication

Multiply.

	a	b	c	d	e
1.	6 ×5	1 ×7	0 ×6	8 ×2	7 ×8
2.	4 ×5	3 ×0	7 ×4	4 ×9	3 ×6
3.	7 ×2	9 ×7	2 ×4	5 ×7	2 ×5

Complete each table.

    a   **b**   **c**

4.   Rule: multiply by 8   Rule: multiply by 7   Rule: multiply by 1

In	Out
5	40
4	
3	
2	

In	Out
2	
7	
5	35
8	

In	Out
3	
5	
7	
9	9

Single Digit Multiplication

Multiply.

	a	b	c	d	e
1.	8 ×9	1 ×8	4 ×8	8 ×5	0 ×8
2.	3 ×8	8 ×6	2 ×8	8 ×7	8 ×1
3.	2 ×8	8 ×4	8 ×2	8 ×1	8 ×8
4.	9 ×8	8 ×0	6 ×8	5 ×8	8 ×3

SCORE ⬭ / 20

Single Digit Multiplication

Fill in the missing number.

	a	b	c	d	e

1.

a. 8 × □ = 64

b. 8 × 5 = □

c. □ × 8 = 48

d. 3 × □ = 24

e. 1 × □ = 8

2.

a. 4 × 8 = □

b. □ × 9 = 72

c. 1 × □ = 8

d. 5 × 8 = □

e. 8 × 3 = □

3.

a. □ × 2 = 16

b. □ × 7 = 56

c. 8 × 6 = □

d. 2 × 8 = □

e. □ × 8 = 40

4.

a. 6 × 8 = □

b. 8 × □ = 32

c. 9 × 8 = □

d. 8 × 3 = □

e. 8 × 0 = □

Single Digit Multiplication

Multiply.

	a	b	c	d	e
1.	9 ×7	3 ×9	9 ×8	9 ×6	4 ×9
2.	9 ×3	9 ×1	5 ×9	9 ×9	2 ×9
3.	9 ×7	9 ×4	8 ×9	9 ×2	9 ×5
4.	0 ×9	9 ×3	6 ×9	9 ×9	9 ×1

Single Digit Multiplication

Multiply.

	a	b	c	d	e
1.	0 ×8	2 ×5	1 ×6	5 ×8	7 ×6
2.	5 ×6	3 ×8	9 ×6	5 ×7	6 ×5
3.	7 ×5	2 ×8	1 ×7	5 ×0	4 ×7

Complete each table.

      a   b   c

4.   Rule: multiply by 9   Rule: multiply by 2   Rule: multiply by 5

In	Out
8	
7	
6	
5	45

In	Out
2	
4	8
6	
8	

In	Out
4	
7	
3	15
9	

SCORE ⬭ **/ 20**

Single Digit Multiplication

Multiply.

	a	b	c	d	e
1.	0 ×7	4 ×3	1 ×5	2 ×6	4 ×7
2.	4 ×8	3 ×6	5 ×5	9 ×6	4 ×2
3.	2 ×5	6 ×6	1 ×4	4 ×5	8 ×6
4.	6 ×5	7 ×3	4 ×4	4 ×6	7 ×9

Number Sentences

A **number sentence** is an equation with numbers.

Identity Property
for multiplication: $1 \times 3 = 3$

Commutative Property
for multiplication: $4 \times 2 = 2 \times 4$

A number sentence can change its look but not change its value.

$$3 \times 8 = 24 \text{ or } 3 \times 8 = 6 \times 4$$

Complete each number sentence.

	a	b	c	d
1.	$1 \times 2 = \boxed{}$	$1 \times 5 = \boxed{}$	$\boxed{} \times 4 = 4$	$\boxed{} \times 9 = 9$
2.	$5 \times 7 = 7 \times \boxed{}$	$4 \times \boxed{} = 3 \times 4$	$\boxed{} \times 3 = 3 \times 5$	$9 \times 4 = \boxed{} \times 9$

Complete the following.

	a	b	c	d
3.	$5 \times 6 = 30$ or $5 \times 6 = 10 \times \boxed{}$	$4 \times 3 = 12$ or $4 \times 3 = 2 \times \boxed{}$	$6 \times 3 = 18$ or $6 \times 3 = 9 \times \boxed{}$	$6 \times 2 = 12$ or $6 \times 2 = 4 \times \boxed{}$
4.	$8 \times 5 = 40$ or $8 \times 5 = 4 \times \boxed{}$	$4 \times 4 = 16$ or $4 \times 4 = 2 \times \boxed{}$	$9 \times 4 = 36$ or $9 \times 4 = 6 \times \boxed{}$	$2 \times 10 = 20$ or $2 \times 10 = 4 \times \boxed{}$

Single Digit Multiplication

Complete the following.

	a	**b**
1.	$7 \times 3 = \boxed{}$ $3 \times 7 = \boxed{}$	$6 \times 5 = \boxed{}$ $5 \times 6 = \boxed{}$
2.	$2 \times 3 = \boxed{}$ $3 \times 2 = \boxed{}$	$4 \times 6 = \boxed{}$ $6 \times 4 = \boxed{}$
3.	$2 \times 9 = \boxed{}$ $9 \times 2 = \boxed{}$	$8 \times 4 = \boxed{}$ $4 \times 8 = \boxed{}$
4.	$7 \times 2 = \boxed{}$ $2 \times 7 = \boxed{}$	$3 \times 6 = \boxed{}$ $6 \times 3 = \boxed{}$
5.	$9 \times 4 = \boxed{}$ $4 \times 9 = \boxed{}$	$8 \times 3 = \boxed{}$ $3 \times 8 = \boxed{}$
6.	$5 \times 2 = \boxed{}$ $2 \times 5 = \boxed{}$	$9 \times 3 = \boxed{}$ $3 \times 9 = \boxed{}$

Check What You Learned

Single Digit Multiplication

Multiply.

	a	b	c	d	e
1.	3 ×6	8 ×2	4 ×9	7 ×9	6 ×6
2.	7 ×7	5 ×5	4 ×3	6 ×8	7 ×4
3.	5 ×9	9 ×8	5 ×6	4 ×2	6 ×3
4.	4 ×5	7 ×2	6 ×5	8 ×6	7 ×8
5.	8 ×5	9 ×7	7 ×3	4 ×6	8 ×9

Fill in the missing numbers.

6.

□ × 8 64	6 × □ 42	□ × 9 54	□ × 4 16	5 × □ 15

NAME _____

Check What You Know

Problem Solving: Single Digit Multiplication

Read the problem carefully and solve. Show your work under each question.

Kevin buys school supplies. He buys markers, pencils, pens, and erasers.

---

1. Pencils come in packages of 6. If Kevin buys 4 packages, how many pencils will he have?

_____ pencils

2. Markers come in packages of 7. If Kevin buys 5 packages, how many markers will he have?

_____ markers

3. Erasers come in boxes of 9. If Kevin buys 8 boxes and gives 3 boxes to his little brother, how many erasers will he have?

_____ erasers

4. Pens come in packages of 8. Kevin wants to know how many pens he will have if he buys 3 packages. How can he write and solve this as an addition problem?

_____ pens

Understanding Multiplication

Read the problem carefully and solve. Show your work under each question.

Dylan makes fruit baskets to give to his family. In each basket, Dylan puts in 3 pears, 5 bananas, and 6 apples.

Helpful Hint

When multiplying, remember that multiplication can be written and solved as an addition problem.

Examples:

6×2 means the same as $6 + 6$

4×3 means the same as $4 + 4 + 4$

---

1. Dylan wrote down 5×2 to find out how many bananas he will need to make 2 fruit baskets. Write and solve the corresponding addition problem.

   _____

2. Dylan wrote down 3×3 to find out how many pears he will need to make 3 fruit baskets. Write and solve the corresponding addition problem.

   _____

3. Dylan wants to know how many apples he will need to make 3 fruit baskets. What multiplication problem should Dylan write to find the answer? Solve the problem.

   _____

Multiplying through 5 × 9

Read the problem carefully and solve. Show your work under each question.

Emilio and Maria each make a photo album. Maria can fit 3 photos on each page of her album. She fills 9 pages. Emilio can fit 4 photos on each page of his album. He fills 7 pages.

> **Helpful Hint**
>
> To solve a multiplication word problem, you need to find:
>
> 1. the number of groups
> 2. the number of items in each group

1. Who has the most photos in their album, Emilio or Maria?

_____ has the most photos.

2. Maria takes all the photos from 3 pages of her album to school. How many photos does she take to school?

_____ photos

3. Emilio adds some photos to his album. He fills 2 more pages. How many photos does Emilio have in his album now?

_____ photos

Single Digit Multiplication

Read the problem carefully and solve. Show your work under each question.

Ella makes necklaces for a craft fair. For each necklace, she uses 4 yellow beads, 7 blue beads, 6 red beads, and 8 green beads.

Helpful Hint

If you know the total number of items in a group and the number of groups, then you can write an equation to help you solve the problem using multiplication:

$3 \times a = 18$

$3 \times 6 = 18$

$a = 6$

---

1. Ella finds 72 green beads in her backpack. She plans to make 9 necklaces with the 72 beads. Write a multiplication equation to find how many beads Ella will use on each necklace. Then, solve.

_____

_____ beads

2. Ella wants to make 8 more necklaces. How many more blue beads will she need? How many more green beads will she need?

_____ blue beads

_____ green beads

Single Digit Multiplication

Read the problem carefully and solve. Show your work under each question.

Ella makes necklaces for a craft fair. For each necklace, she uses 4 yellow beads, 7 blue beads, 6 red beads, and 8 green beads.

1. To make 6 necklaces, how many red beads does Ella use?

_____ red beads

2. Ella wants to make 5 extra necklaces for her friends. But, she is out of yellow beads. How many yellow beads will she need to buy to make the necklaces?

_____ yellow beads

3. Ella's necklaces are a big hit. She needs to make 7 more during the craft fair. How many more beads in each color will she need?

_____ yellow beads

_____ blue beads

_____ red beads

_____ green beads

Single Digit Multiplication

Solve each problem. Show your work under each question.

1. Steven wants to buy 6 pieces of bubblegum. Each piece costs 5 cents. How much will he have to pay for the bubblegum?

   Steven wants to buy _____ pieces of bubblegum.

   One piece of bubblegum costs _____ cents.

   Steven will have to pay _____ cents total.

2. There are 7 girls on stage. Each girl is holding 9 flowers. How many flowers are there in all?

   There are _____ girls.

   Each girl is holding _____ flowers.

   There are _____ flowers in all.

Single Digit Multiplication

Solve each problem. Show your work under each question.

1. There are 4 rows of desks. There are 8 desks in each row. How many desks are there in all?

   There are _____ rows of desks.

   There are _____ desks in each row.

   There are _____ desks in all.

2. Sara earns 4 dollars a day babysitting her cousin. If Sara babysits for 5 days two weeks in a row, how much money will she earn?

   Sara will earn _____ dollars.

3. Jose scored 16 total points during a basketball game. He scored the same number of points in each of the 4 quarters. Write a multiplication equation to find how many points he scored each quarter. Then, solve.

   _____

   He scored _____ points each quarter.

Number Sentences

Read the problem carefully and solve. Show your work under each question.

Mr. Glenn splits his students into pairs. Each pair of students has to count the number of crayons they brought to class. Next, they will write a number sentence that compares the number of crayons they brought to class.

1. Helen organized her crayons into 3 groups of 7 crayons. She then organized her crayons into 7 equal groups. Complete the number sentence to find out how many crayons are in each of the 7 groups.

   $3 \times 7 = 7 \times \boxed{}$

2. Maria brought 4 groups of 2 crayons to class. Fred reorganized Maria's crayons into 2 equal groups of crayons. Complete the number sentence to show how many crayons are in the two groups.

   $4 \times 2 = 2 \times \boxed{}$

3. Greg put 1 crayon into 6 different groups. Complete the number sentence to find out how many crayons Gregg has total.

   $6 \times 1 = \boxed{}$

Check What You Learned

Problem Solving: Single Digit Multiplication

Read the problem carefully and solve. Show your work under each question.

The students at P.S. 134 are having a book sale. They are arranging the books into categories and stacking them on tables.

1. Josh sorted books about sports. When he was finished, he had 8 stacks of 6 books each. Kate brought over 6 more stacks with 8 books each. How many sports books in all were at the sale?

_____ sports books

2. The largest category of books was fiction. Rebecca had 2 stacks with 8 books in each stack. How many fiction books were at the sale?

_____ fiction books

3. The book sale was in the gym. The students set up tables into 9 rows with 4 tables in each row. What was the total number of tables in the gym?

_____ tables

4. The customers were excited by the sale. They lined up to pay for their books. There were 5 lines with 7 customers in each line. How many customers were waiting to pay?

_____ customers

Mid-Test Chapters 1–2

Fill in the missing number.

	a	**b**	**c**	**d**	**e**

1.

a.
$$
\begin{array}{r}
7 \\
\times \;\boxed{} \\
\hline
14
\end{array}
$$

b.
$$
\begin{array}{r}
9 \\
\times \; 7 \\
\hline
\boxed{}
\end{array}
$$

c.
$$
\begin{array}{r}
\boxed{} \\
\times \; 4 \\
\hline
8
\end{array}
$$

d.
$$
\begin{array}{r}
5 \\
\times \; 7 \\
\hline
\boxed{}
\end{array}
$$

e.
$$
\begin{array}{r}
\boxed{} \\
\times \; 5 \\
\hline
10
\end{array}
$$

2.

a.
$$
\begin{array}{r}
\boxed{} \\
\times \; 6 \\
\hline
36
\end{array}
$$

b.
$$
\begin{array}{r}
8 \\
\times \; 5 \\
\hline
\boxed{}
\end{array}
$$

c.
$$
\begin{array}{r}
5 \\
\times \;\boxed{} \\
\hline
25
\end{array}
$$

d.
$$
\begin{array}{r}
6 \\
\times \;\boxed{} \\
\hline
48
\end{array}
$$

e.
$$
\begin{array}{r}
9 \\
\times \; 4 \\
\hline
\boxed{}
\end{array}
$$

3.

a.
$$
\begin{array}{r}
3 \\
\times \;\boxed{} \\
\hline
18
\end{array}
$$

b.
$$
\begin{array}{r}
\boxed{} \\
\times \; 9 \\
\hline
36
\end{array}
$$

c.
$$
\begin{array}{r}
7 \\
\times \; 4 \\
\hline
\boxed{}
\end{array}
$$

d.
$$
\begin{array}{r}
3 \\
\times \;\boxed{} \\
\hline
3
\end{array}
$$

e.
$$
\begin{array}{r}
4 \\
\times \;\boxed{} \\
\hline
20
\end{array}
$$

4.

a.
$$
\begin{array}{r}
7 \\
\times \; 8 \\
\hline
\boxed{}
\end{array}
$$

b.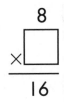
$$
\begin{array}{r}
8 \\
\times \;\boxed{} \\
\hline
16
\end{array}
$$

c.
$$
\begin{array}{r}
1 \\
\times \;\boxed{} \\
\hline
6
\end{array}
$$

d.
$$
\begin{array}{r}
\boxed{} \\
\times \; 7 \\
\hline
7
\end{array}
$$

e.
$$
\begin{array}{r}
6 \\
\times \; 5 \\
\hline
\boxed{}
\end{array}
$$

Mid-Test Chapters 1–2

Multiply.

	a	b	c	d	e
5.	4 ×9	3 ×4	3 ×7	2 ×5	2 ×4
6.	4 ×8	2 ×0	3 ×2	2 ×8	4 ×7
7.	2 ×6	3 ×1	4 ×1	4 ×6	2 ×4

Complete each table.

a
8. Rule: multiply by 5

In	Out
9	
4	20
1	
8	

b
Rule: multiply by 3

In	Out
0	
7	
2	
8	24

c
Rule: multiply by 6

In	Out
6	
3	
1	6
9	

Mid-Test Chapters 1–2

Read the problem carefully and solve. Show your work under each question.

The students at Kyle's school are having a bake sale. Kyle and his friends arrange the baked goods on the tables according to category.

---

9. At the cookie table, there are 2 lines with 9 customers in each line. How many customers were waiting to buy cookies?

_____ customers

10. Ming sorted 56 brownies into stacks. She made 8 stacks with the same number of brownies in each stack. Write a multiplication equation to find how many brownies are in each stack. Then, solve.

_____

_____ brownies

11. Kyle was selling cakes for $5 each. Kyle's teacher bought 5 cakes for a party. How much did his teacher pay for the cakes?

_____ dollars

12. When the sale was over, the students counted the money. Bruno counted 5 five-dollar bills. Leo counted 4 five-dollar bills. How much money did they count altogether?

_____ dollars

NAME _____

Check What You Know

Multiplying 2 Digits by 1 Digit

Multiply.

	a	b	c	d	e
1.	26 × 3	24 × 4	47 × 2	14 × 6	53 × 4
2.	39 × 2	14 × 7	25 × 3	13 × 5	37 × 2
3.	48 × 2	23 × 4	35 × 2	12 × 8	24 × 3
4.	13 × 6	18 × 5	29 × 3	17 × 5	49 × 2
5.	16 × 6	36 × 2	18 × 3	15 × 6	27 × 3
6.	13 × 7	28 × 3	19 × 5	46 × 2	16 × 5

Multiplying 2 Digits by 1 Digit

	Multiply 2 ones by 3.	Multiply 8 tens by 3.		

```
    82            82            82            82       factor
  ×  3          ×  3          ×  3          ×  3       factor
  ─────         ─────         ─────         ─────
                   6             6             6    >  Add.
                             2 4 0         +2 4 0
                                           ─────
                                            2 4 6     product
```

Multiply. Show your work.

	a	b	c	d	e
1.	73 × 2 ── 6 +140 ──── 146	14 × 2	90 × 5	45 × 1	33 × 3
2.	22 × 4	86 × 1	52 × 4	31 × 5	46 × 1
3.	19 × 1	21 × 4	43 × 3	27 × 1	91 × 5
4.	56 × 1	52 × 2	63 × 3	73 × 1	62 × 2

Multiplication and Place Value

Use place value to multiply by multiples of 10.

$9 \times 40 = 9$ ones $\times 4$ tens   Multiply 9 ones by 4 tens.

9×4 tens $= 36$ tens $= 360$

$9 \times 40 = 360$

Multiply.

	a	b	c	d	e
1.	10×4	20×6	40×2	50×9	40×6
2.	80×9	60×3	30×8	90×2	70×3
3.	50×4	80×5	60×7	90×3	20×5
4.	60×6	70×2	80×8	40×5	50×6

Multiplication and Place Value

Multiply.

	a	b	c	d	e
1.	50 × 6	70 × 3	80 × 5	60 × 7	30 × 4
2.	90 × 9	50 × 3	60 × 8	10 × 8	20 × 3
3.	20 × 4	10 × 5	90 × 8	30 × 7	60 × 5
4.	10 × 9	30 × 8	40 × 7	60 × 7	40 × 7
5.	80 × 8	90 × 6	30 × 3	70 × 4	10 × 6

Multiplication Practice

Multiply.

	a	b	c	d	e
1.	23×2	71×1	12×4	33×2	10×7
2.	44×2	43×2	90×1	22×4	12×3
3.	11×9	75×1	11×6	30×3	10×4
4.	11×7	10×2	33×0	13×3	20×3
5.	10×2	41×2	13×2	40×2	30×2

Multiplication Practice

Multiply.

	a	b	c	d	e
1.	$\begin{array}{r} 24 \\ \times\ 2 \\ \hline \end{array}$	$\begin{array}{r} 14 \\ \times\ 2 \\ \hline \end{array}$	$\begin{array}{r} 42 \\ \times\ 2 \\ \hline \end{array}$	$\begin{array}{r} 31 \\ \times\ 2 \\ \hline \end{array}$	$\begin{array}{r} 11 \\ \times\ 5 \\ \hline \end{array}$
2.	$\begin{array}{r} 30 \\ \times\ 1 \\ \hline \end{array}$	$\begin{array}{r} 11 \\ \times\ 7 \\ \hline \end{array}$	$\begin{array}{r} 25 \\ \times\ 1 \\ \hline \end{array}$	$\begin{array}{r} 42 \\ \times\ 0 \\ \hline \end{array}$	$\begin{array}{r} 22 \\ \times\ 3 \\ \hline \end{array}$
3.	$\begin{array}{r} 10 \\ \times\ 1 \\ \hline \end{array}$	$\begin{array}{r} 14 \\ \times\ 0 \\ \hline \end{array}$	$\begin{array}{r} 10 \\ \times\ 5 \\ \hline \end{array}$	$\begin{array}{r} 31 \\ \times\ 3 \\ \hline \end{array}$	$\begin{array}{r} 12 \\ \times\ 3 \\ \hline \end{array}$
4.	$\begin{array}{r} 20 \\ \times\ 4 \\ \hline \end{array}$	$\begin{array}{r} 10 \\ \times\ 7 \\ \hline \end{array}$	$\begin{array}{r} 15 \\ \times\ 1 \\ \hline \end{array}$	$\begin{array}{r} 20 \\ \times\ 3 \\ \hline \end{array}$	$\begin{array}{r} 11 \\ \times\ 3 \\ \hline \end{array}$
5.	$\begin{array}{r} 60 \\ \times\ 1 \\ \hline \end{array}$	$\begin{array}{r} 43 \\ \times\ 2 \\ \hline \end{array}$	$\begin{array}{r} 33 \\ \times\ 3 \\ \hline \end{array}$	$\begin{array}{r} 11 \\ \times\ 9 \\ \hline \end{array}$	$\begin{array}{r} 28 \\ \times\ 0 \\ \hline \end{array}$

Multiplication Practice

Multiply.

	a	b	c	d	e
1.	32 × 3	21 × 4	33 × 2	30 × 3	21 × 2
2.	43 × 2	20 × 3	11 × 4	34 × 2	21 × 3
3.	33 × 3	24 × 2	22 × 4	40 × 2	32 × 2
4.	13 × 3	22 × 2	20 × 4	23 × 2	11 × 3
5.	41 × 2	31 × 3	44 × 2	23 × 3	12 × 4

Multiplying 2 Digits by 1 Digit (with renaming)

Multiply 6 ones by 3.

Multiply 2 tens by 3. Add the 1 ten.

$$26 \\ \times \ 3$$

$$\begin{matrix} 1 \\ 26 \\ \times \ 3 \\ \hline 8 \end{matrix}$$

$$3 \times 6 = 18 = 10 + 8$$

$$3 \times 20 = 60$$

$$\begin{matrix} 1 \\ 26 \\ \times \ 3 \\ \hline 78 \end{matrix}$$

$$60 + 10 = 70$$

$$\begin{matrix} 26 \ \longleftarrow \ \text{factor} \\ \times \ 3 \ \longleftarrow \ \text{factor} \\ \hline 78 \ \longleftarrow \ \text{product} \end{matrix}$$

Multiply.

	a	**b**	**c**	**d**	**e**
1.	$\begin{matrix} 37 \\ \times \ 2 \\ \hline 74 \end{matrix}$	$\begin{matrix} 19 \\ \times \ 5 \\ \hline \end{matrix}$	$\begin{matrix} 45 \\ \times \ 2 \\ \hline \end{matrix}$	$\begin{matrix} 38 \\ \times \ 2 \\ \hline \end{matrix}$	$\begin{matrix} 25 \\ \times \ 3 \\ \hline \end{matrix}$
2.	$\begin{matrix} 14 \\ \times \ 4 \\ \hline \end{matrix}$	$\begin{matrix} 47 \\ \times \ 2 \\ \hline \end{matrix}$	$\begin{matrix} 28 \\ \times \ 3 \\ \hline \end{matrix}$	$\begin{matrix} 13 \\ \times \ 4 \\ \hline \end{matrix}$	$\begin{matrix} 23 \\ \times \ 4 \\ \hline \end{matrix}$
3.	$\begin{matrix} 26 \\ \times \ 2 \\ \hline \end{matrix}$	$\begin{matrix} 36 \\ \times \ 2 \\ \hline \end{matrix}$	$\begin{matrix} 13 \\ \times \ 5 \\ \hline \end{matrix}$	$\begin{matrix} 15 \\ \times \ 3 \\ \hline \end{matrix}$	$\begin{matrix} 27 \\ \times \ 2 \\ \hline \end{matrix}$

Multiplying 2 Digits by 1 Digit (with renaming)

Multiply.

	a	b	c	d	e
1.	12 × 5	24 × 4	18 × 5	15 × 5	17 × 3
2.	24 × 3	39 × 2	14 × 5	16 × 2	27 × 3
3.	15 × 4	29 × 2	26 × 3	36 × 2	17 × 5
4.	35 × 2	25 × 2	28 × 2	14 × 3	17 × 4
5.	29 × 3	19 × 3	23 × 4	38 × 2	13 × 6

Multiplication Practice

Multiply.

	a	b	c	d	e
1.	72 × 5	38 × 4	29 × 5	27 × 4	25 × 5
2.	54 × 3	96 × 3	84 × 4	92 × 5	47 × 3
3.	45 × 3	23 × 5	86 × 3	73 × 5	22 × 5
4.	64 × 3	93 × 4	86 × 5	43 × 4	38 × 3

SCORE ◯ **/ 20**

Multiplication Practice

Multiply.

	a	b	c	d	e
1.	36 × 4	86 × 2	56 × 4	74 × 4	34 × 3
2.	28 × 5	37 × 3	46 × 4	23 × 5	83 × 4
3.	44 × 3	59 × 3	82 × 5	74 × 5	63 × 4
4.	47 × 4	85 × 3	37 × 6	19 × 9	84 × 5

Multiplication Practice

Multiply.

	a	b	c	d	e
1.	73 $\times$ 4	25 $\times$ 2	36 $\times$ 3	52 $\times$ 5	23 $\times$ 4
2.	19 $\times$ 2	26 $\times$ 2	68 $\times$ 3	54 $\times$ 5	47 $\times$ 8
3.	32 $\times$ 9	48 $\times$ 8	52 $\times$ 3	34 $\times$ 4	17 $\times$ 5
4.	66 $\times$ 3	45 $\times$ 5	66 $\times$ 5	19 $\times$ 9	38 $\times$ 9
5.	55 $\times$ 3	64 $\times$ 8	83 $\times$ 5	49 $\times$ 7	50 $\times$ 9

Multiplication Practice

Multiply.

	a	b	c	d	e
1.	42 × 5	33 × 4	22 × 5	74 × 3	86 × 6
2.	60 × 6	17 × 3	48 × 9	75 × 3	60 × 9
3.	96 × 5	31 × 9	77 × 4	82 × 3	96 × 3
4.	40 × 7	79 × 2	52 × 5	46 × 3	27 × 8
5.	39 × 6	43 × 7	83 × 2	24 × 8	55 × 3

Multiplication Practice

Multiply.

	a	b	c	d	e
1.	16 × 3	28 × 2	34 × 7	22 × 9	17 × 6
2.	74 × 6	34 × 9	28 × 6	63 × 1	17 × 4
3.	36 × 4	27 × 8	52 × 2	73 × 7	65 × 9
4.	26 × 5	84 × 8	92 × 3	58 × 4	36 × 8

Multiplication Practice

Multiply.

	a	b	c	d	e
1.	42 × 7	65 × 5	87 × 2	49 × 6	70 × 5
2.	46 × 7	28 × 9	37 × 2	97 × 1	52 × 4
3.	16 × 5	76 × 2	73 × 3	56 × 8	75 × 4
4.	93 × 6	28 × 3	45 × 4	18 × 6	12 × 9

Multiplication Practice

Multiply.

	a	b	c	d	e
1.	86 × 3	72 × 5	67 × 4	91 × 9	22 × 7
2.	51 × 2	38 × 7	43 × 8	29 × 1	18 × 6
3.	57 × 6	16 × 9	82 × 5	33 × 3	17 × 8
4.	13 × 6	10 × 7	73 × 5	64 × 8	31 × 9

SCORE ⬭ **/ 20**

Multiplication Practice

Multiply.

	a	b	c	d	e
1.	$\begin{array}{r} 65 \\ \times\ 5 \\ \hline \end{array}$	$\begin{array}{r} 46 \\ \times\ 1 \\ \hline \end{array}$	$\begin{array}{r} 29 \\ \times\ 5 \\ \hline \end{array}$	$\begin{array}{r} 28 \\ \times\ 7 \\ \hline \end{array}$	$\begin{array}{r} 36 \\ \times\ 3 \\ \hline \end{array}$
2.	$\begin{array}{r} 84 \\ \times\ 3 \\ \hline \end{array}$	$\begin{array}{r} 69 \\ \times\ 7 \\ \hline \end{array}$	$\begin{array}{r} 16 \\ \times\ 5 \\ \hline \end{array}$	$\begin{array}{r} 44 \\ \times\ 2 \\ \hline \end{array}$	$\begin{array}{r} 39 \\ \times\ 1 \\ \hline \end{array}$
3.	$\begin{array}{r} 87 \\ \times\ 6 \\ \hline \end{array}$	$\begin{array}{r} 17 \\ \times\ 3 \\ \hline \end{array}$	$\begin{array}{r} 34 \\ \times\ 5 \\ \hline \end{array}$	$\begin{array}{r} 53 \\ \times\ 2 \\ \hline \end{array}$	$\begin{array}{r} 39 \\ \times\ 8 \\ \hline \end{array}$
4.	$\begin{array}{r} 15 \\ \times\ 4 \\ \hline \end{array}$	$\begin{array}{r} 62 \\ \times\ 3 \\ \hline \end{array}$	$\begin{array}{r} 19 \\ \times\ 3 \\ \hline \end{array}$	$\begin{array}{r} 22 \\ \times\ 4 \\ \hline \end{array}$	$\begin{array}{r} 23 \\ \times\ 4 \\ \hline \end{array}$

Multiplication Practice

Multiply.

	a	b	c	d	e
1.	31 × 5	42 × 2	36 × 1	52 × 4	83 × 3
2.	39 × 1	41 × 4	52 × 2	28 × 1	13 × 3
3.	54 × 2	17 × 1	29 × 0	23 × 3	42 × 4
4.	61 × 5	72 × 3	14 × 2	86 × 1	47 × 1
5.	83 × 2	42 × 3	69 × 3	11 × 5	61 × 2

Multiplication Practice

Multiply.

	a	b	c	d	e
1.	75 × 1	30 × 5	41 × 5	92 × 3	58 × 1
2.	13 × 2	10 × 5	23 × 2	42 × 1	82 × 4
3.	31 × 4	22 × 3	33 × 2	43 × 3	52 × 3
4.	92 × 2	54 × 1	14 × 1	52 × 3	17 × 0
5.	34 × 2	30 × 4	65 × 1	23 × 2	11 × 4

Multiplication Practice

Multiply.

	a	b	c	d	e
1.	37 × 4	48 × 3	23 × 6	97 × 2	47 × 5
2.	76 × 2	59 × 4	34 × 6	38 × 5	48 × 2
3.	45 × 6	67 × 3	43 × 4	85 × 2	39 × 5
4.	64 × 3	83 × 6	45 × 3	63 × 5	93 × 4
5.	86 × 2	73 × 5	66 × 4	25 × 6	74 × 3

Multiplication Practice

Multiply.

	a	b	c	d	e
1.	13 × 5	38 × 2	48 × 2	19 × 4	29 × 3
2.	14 × 8	15 × 6	36 × 3	39 × 2	27 × 4
3.	28 × 3	47 × 2	16 × 9	15 × 5	13 × 7
4.	17 × 6	25 × 4	24 × 3	45 × 2	16 × 8
5.	14 × 7	29 × 2	16 × 4	37 × 3	16 × 5

Multiplication Practice

Multiply.

	a	b	c	d	e
1.	26 × 3	64 × 5	65 × 5	34 × 8	47 × 6
2.	43 × 8	57 × 6	98 × 2	35 × 4	76 × 3
3.	46 × 7	85 × 3	35 × 8	23 × 9	62 × 5
4.	42 × 6	73 × 4	82 × 5	67 × 3	27 × 8
5.	49 × 7	88 × 2	36 × 9	53 × 6	83 × 4

Multiplication Practice

Multiply.

	a	b	c	d	e
1.	84 × 5	35 × 7	64 × 7	43 × 9	28 × 6
2.	63 × 8	57 × 4	55 × 9	43 × 6	92 × 8
3.	42 × 9	85 × 6	53 × 4	74 × 8	83 × 5
4.	65 × 7	87 × 3	49 × 6	23 × 9	86 × 4
5.	35 × 8	82 × 5	32 × 9	46 × 6	89 × 2

Check What You Learned

Multiplying 2 Digits by 1 Digit

Multiply.

	a	**b**	**c**	**d**	**e**
1.	76 × 4	23 × 6	57 × 6	48 × 8	73 × 9
2.	49 × 8	64 × 5	87 × 9	43 × 7	88 × 3
3.	73 × 6	54 × 8	69 × 5	74 × 9	39 × 7
4.	83 × 9	45 × 6	75 × 8	62 × 7	28 × 9
5.	52 × 8	63 × 5	77 × 3	38 × 9	97 × 2
6.	48 × 7	53 × 9	29 × 7	37 × 8	82 × 7

Check What You Know

Problem Solving: Multiplying 2 Digits by 1 Digit

Read the problem carefully and solve. Show your work under each question.

Dwight and Juanita go to the post office to buy stamps. Stamps at the post office cost 5 cents, 33 cents, or 46 cents.

1. Dwight buys 23 of the 5-cent stamps. How much does this cost?

_____ cents

2. Juanita buys 59 of the 5-cent stamps. How much does this cost?

_____ cents

3. The 46-cent stamps are for mailing letters. Dwight wants to buy 3 of these stamps to mail birthday cards. In cents, how much does this cost?

_____ cents

4. The 33-cent stamps are for mailing postcards. Juanita buys 4 of these stamps to mail postcards from a recent trip. She also buys 1 46-cent stamp to mail a letter. In cents, how much does Juanita spend total?

_____ cents

Multiplying 2 Digits by 1 Digit

Read the problem carefully and solve. Show your work under each question.

David shops for clothes at the local department store, which is having a sale. A pair of pants costs $42, a shirt costs $21, and a sweater costs $51.

Helpful Hint

To multiply a 2-digit number by a 1-digit number, multiply the ones, then the tens. Remember to carry the dollar sign to your answer.

Example:

$$\begin{array}{r} \$94 \\ \times \quad 2 \\ \hline \$188 \end{array}$$

1. David wants to buy 4 shirts. How much does this cost?

_____

2. David wants to buy 4 pairs of pants. How much does this cost?

_____

3. David wants to buy 5 sweaters. How much does this cost?

_____

Multiplying 2 Digits by 1 Digit

Read the problem carefully and solve. Show your work under each question.

Roger and his friend Aaron like to go mountain biking. They keep track of the total miles they bike each week. Roger bikes 32 miles each week. Aaron bikes 23 miles each week.

1. After 3 weeks, how many miles has Roger biked in total?

_____ miles

2. Aaron calculates the total number of miles he biked in 3 weeks. How many miles did he bike?

_____ miles

3. Roger and Aaron bike for another 2 weeks. How many miles did each of them bike during those two weeks?

Roger biked _____ miles.

Aaron biked _____ miles.

Multiplying 2 Digits by 1 Digit (with renaming)

Read the problem carefully and solve. Show your work under each question.

Carrie works for a catering company that sells large food platters. The chart on the right shows how many people each platter can feed.

Platter	Number of Meals
Sandwich	28
Salad	37
Pasta	46

Helpful Hint

Rename the top number in a multiplication problem if needed.

Example:

$$\begin{array}{r} \overset{1}{2\,6} \\ \times\ \ 3 \\ \hline 7\,8 \end{array}$$

1. The local bank orders 2 sandwich platters. How many people can these platters feed?

   _____ people

2. The convention center orders 3 pasta platters. How many people can these platters feed?

   _____ people

3. The teachers at the elementary school order 4 salad platters. How many people can these platters feed?

   _____ people

SCORE [ ] / 3

Multiplication Practice

Read the problem carefully and solve. Show your work under each question.

Asa, Juan, and Suzie are students at the elementary school. They help Ms. Hardy, the school librarian, in the library.

---

1. The 3 students each take 19 books from the book return and put them back on the shelves. How many books altogether did they put back on the shelves?

_____ books

2. Ms. Hardy asks Juan to put this month's new books on display. There are 6 stacks of new books that Ms. Hardy wants to put on display. There are 28 books in each stack. How many new books are there?

_____ new books

3. Suzie is going to move 4 shelves of mystery books and 5 shelves of fiction books to a different part of the library. There are 32 books on each shelf. How many books will Suzie move?

_____ books

Multiplication Practice

Solve each problem. Show your work under each question.

1. There are 40 chicken farms near an Ohio town. If each farm has 9 barns, how
many total barns are there?

There are _____ total barns.

2. Mr. Ferris has a canoe rental business. Over the weekend, he rented 47 canoes.
A canoe holds 3 people. If each canoe was full, how many people did Mr. Ferris
rent to over the weekend?

Mr. Ferris rented to _____ people.

3. The school planned for 92 students to attend the school dance. The school bought
4 slices of pizza for each student. How many slices did the school buy?

The school bought _____ slices.

Multiplication Practice

Solve each problem. Show your work under each question.

1. The pool opened on Memorial Day. Ninety-four people showed up. The pool manager gave out 2 vouchers to each person for free drinks. How many vouchers did the pool manager give out?

The manager gave out _____ vouchers.

2. In the Sumton community, there are 56 houses. If there are 3 children living in each house, how many children live in houses in Sumton?

There are _____ children living in houses in Sumton.

3. Deon and Denise are saving up to buy a computer game. If they put 23 dollars a week in the bank, how much money will they have in 5 weeks?

They will have _____ dollars.

Multiplication Practice

Solve each problem. Show your work under each question.

1. Xavier loves to eat pears. He ate 2 a day for 48 days. How many pears did Xavier eat?

   Xavier ate _____ pears.

2. Clayton keeps pet mice. If his 33 mice have 4 babies each, how many mice will Clayton have in all?

   Clayton will have _____ mice.

3. A class of 55 students went on a field trip to collect seashells. If the students collected 5 shells each, how many shells did they collect?

   The students collected _____ shells.

Multiplication Practice

Solve each problem. Show your work under each question.

1. John bought four 23-cent stamps. How many cents did John spend on stamps?

The stamps cost _____ cents.

2. A clown had 13 balloons that he sold at a carnival for 5 cents each. If he sold all 13 balloons, how much money did he make?

The clown made _____ cents.

3. The movie rental store charges 3 dollars to rent each movie. Miss Padilla rents 5 movies. How much will the movie rental store charge her?

The movie rental store will charge Miss Padilla _____ dollars.

Check What You Learned

Problem Solving: Multiplying 2 Digits by 1 Digit

Read the problem carefully and solve. Show your work under each question.

Erin is having a yard sale. She is selling books for $3, toys for $5, and dishes for $2.

1. Lee buys 14 toys. How much does this cost?

_____

2. Erin's teacher, Mr. Garcia, buys 8 animal books and 16 fiction books for his classroom. How much does this cost?

_____

3. Ms. Kwan lives next door to Erin. She buys 23 dishes at the yard sale. How much does this cost?

_____

4. Kim works at the youth center. She buys 17 toys at the yard sale. How much does this cost?

_____

Final Test Chapters 1–4

Multiply.

	a	b	c	d	e
1.	13 × 5	7 ×2	10 × 0	81 × 4	42 × 2
2.	52 × 3	76 × 5	41 × 5	3 ×2	14 × 3
3.	45 × 5	93 × 3	42 × 3	33 × 2	10 × 5
4.	51 × 2	91 × 1	17 × 5	31 × 2	25 × 5
5.	32 × 5	8 ×7	5 ×9	4 ×0	38 × 1
6.	6 ×9	4 ×7	22 × 1	19 × 3	83 × 2
7.	6 ×5	53 × 3	18 × 4	8 ×6	13 × 2
8.	7 ×4	5 ×0	3 ×2	8 ×2	56 × 2

Final Test Chapters 1–4

Multiply.

	a	b	c	d	e
9.	1 ×5	9 ×9	3 ×2	5 ×4	6 ×3
10.	9 ×7	5 ×2	6 ×1	8 ×2	5 ×7
11.	6 ×5	8 ×3	4 ×3	0 ×8	6 ×2
12.	13 × 2	23 × 4	17 × 5	42 × 1	18 × 0
13.	54 × 2	96 × 2	53 × 3	33 × 2	11 × 5

Complete each table.

a   b   c

14. Rule: multiply by 4   Rule: multiply by 8   Rule: multiply by 7

In	Out
1	
5	20
7	
8	

In	Out
3	24
6	
4	
8	

In	Out
4	
0	
7	49
1	

Final Test Chapters 1-4

Multiply.

	a	b	c	d	e
15.	2 ×0	5 ×1	4 ×3	0 ×2	5 ×6
16.	7 ×2	9 ×3	8 ×8	6 ×3	4 ×5
17.	6 ×6	3 ×9	1 ×7	5 ×3	2 ×6
18.	3 ×0	4 ×7	6 ×9	4 ×4	5 ×1
19.	7 ×4	3 ×7	2 ×3	4 ×2	9 ×1
20.	20 × 4	14 × 3	29 × 3	32 × 4	96 × 2
21.	46 × 4	72 × 1	61 × 3	70 × 2	52 × 4
22.	21 × 5	15 × 3	31 × 4	90 × 2	56 × 3

FINAL TEST CHAPTERS 1-4

Solve each problem.

23. Kiri has 15 apples to share equally with 5 friends. Write a multiplication equation to find how many apples Kiri gave to each friend. Then, solve.

_____   _____ apples.

24. Each of Mr. Black's 4 daughters needs new shoes. Each pair of shoes will cost 29 dollars. How much money will Mr. Black spend on all 4 pairs of shoes?

Mr. Black will spend _____ dollars on the 4 pairs of shoes.

25. There are 30 students in each classroom. If there are 5 classrooms, how many total students are there?

There are a total of _____ students.

26. There are 7 friends that each have 2 dollars. How much money do the 7 friends have?

The friends have a total of _____ dollars.

27. Write the rule for this table.

In	Out
4	16
6	24
8	32
9	36

_____

Final Test Chapters 1–4

Solve each problem. Show your work under each question.

28. Gary read 3 books with 56 pages each. How many pages did he read in all?

There are _____ pages in each book.

Gary read _____ books.

Gary read _____ pages in all.

29. There are 5 classes at a school. Each class has 32 students. How many students are at the school?

There are _____ students in each class.

There are _____ classes.

There are _____ students in the school.

30. Yolanda bought 4 boxes of cookies for a party. If each box has 24 cookies, how many cookies does she have in all?

Each box has _____ cookies.

Yolanda bought _____ boxes of cookies.

Yolanda bought a total of _____ cookies.

31. During a football game, 2 teams play against each other. There are 11 football players on the field for each team. How many football players are on the field during a football game?

There are _____ football players on the field.

Scoring Record for Pretests, Posttests, Mid-Test, and Final Test

Pretests, Posttests, Mid-Test, and Final Test	Your Score	Performance			
		Excellent	Very Good	Fair	Needs Improvement
Chapter 1 Pretest	____ of 30	28–30	24–27	18–23	17 or fewer
Chapter 1 Posttest	____ of 30	28–30	24–27	18–23	17 or fewer
Chapter 2 Pretest	____ of 4	4	3	2	1
Chapter 2 Posttest	____ of 4	4	3	2	1
Chapter 3 Pretest	____ of 30	28–30	24–27	18–23	17 or fewer
Chapter 3 Posttest	____ of 30	28–30	24–27	18–23	17 or fewer
Chapter 4 Pretest	____ of 4	4	3	2	1
Chapter 4 Posttest	____ of 4	4	3	2	1
Mid-Test	____ of 49	47–49	40–46	30–39	29 or fewer
Final Test	____ of 130	124–130	105–123	79–104	78 or fewer

Record your test score in the Your Score column. See where your score falls in the Performance columns. Your score is based on the total number of required responses. If your score is fair or needs improvement, review the chapter material.

Answer Key

Page 5

Check What You Know
Single Digit Multiplication

Multiply.

	a	b	c	d	e
1.	2 ×0 = 0	5 ×1 = 5	4 ×3 = 12	0 ×2 = 0	5 ×6 = 30
2.	7 ×2 = 14	9 ×3 = 27	8 ×8 = 64	6 ×3 = 18	4 ×5 = 20
3.	6 ×6 = 36	3 ×9 = 27	1 ×7 = 7	5 ×3 = 15	2 ×6 = 12
4.	3 ×0 = 0	4 ×7 = 28	6 ×9 = 54	4 ×4 = 16	5 ×1 = 5
5.	7 ×4 = 28	3 ×7 = 21	2 ×3 = 6	4 ×2 = 8	9 ×1 = 9

Fill in the missing number.

6.
- [3] ×8 = 24
- 5 ×[4] = 20
- 2 ×[2] = 4
- [2] ×9 = 18
- 6 ×[5] = 30

Spectrum Multiplication
Grade 3

Chapter 1
Single Digit Multiplication

5

Page 6

Understanding Multiplication

two times seven
2 × 7 means 7 + 7

7 factor 7
× 2 factor + 7
14 product 14

five times three
5 × 3 means 5 + 5 + 5

5 factor 5
× 3 factor + 5
15 product 15

Multiply. Write the corresponding addition problem next to each multiplication problem.

	a	b	c
1.	3 ×3 = 6	3 = 3	7 ×2 = 14	+7 = 14	6 ×2 = 12	+6 = 12
2.	2 ×2 = 4	+2 = 4	1 ×2 = 2	+1 = 2	5 ×3 = 15	+5 = 15
3.	2 ×3 = 6	+2 = 6	1 ×3 = 3	+1 = 3	4 ×3 = 12	+4 = 12
4.	4 ×4 = 16	+4 = 16	1 ×4 = 4	+1 = 4	5 ×4 = 20	+5 = 20

Spectrum Multiplication
Grade 3

Chapter 1
Single Digit Multiplication

6

Page 7

Understanding Multiplication

Multiply. Write the corresponding addition problem next to each multiplication problem.

	a	b	c
1.	9 ×2 = 18	+9 = 18	8 ×2 = 16	+8 = 16	6 ×3 = 18	+6 = 18
2.	3 ×3 = 9	+3 = 9	7 ×3 = 21	+7 = 21	2 ×4 = 8	+2 = 8
3.	9 ×4 = 36	+9 = 36	8 ×4 = 32	+8 = 32	3 ×4 = 12	+3 = 12
4.	4 ×2 = 8	+4 = 8	5 ×2 = 10	+5 = 10	8 ×3 = 24	+8 = 24

Spectrum Multiplication
Grade 3

Chapter 1
Single Digit Multiplication

7

Page 8

Multiplying through 5 × 9

Multiply.

	a	b	c	d	e
1.	5 ×0 = 0	3 ×9 = 27	6 ×5 = 30	1 ×4 = 4	5 ×1 = 5
2.	9 ×2 = 18	8 ×5 = 40	5 ×8 = 40	0 ×0 = 0	2 ×9 = 18
3.	4 ×6 = 24	7 ×3 = 21	6 ×1 = 6	7 ×2 = 14	3 ×5 = 15
4.	6 ×2 = 12	5 ×5 = 25	9 ×1 = 9	2 ×4 = 8	3 ×7 = 21

Spectrum Multiplication
Grade 3

Chapter 1
Single Digit Multiplication

8

Page 9

Multiplying through 5 × 9

Multiply.

	a	b	c	d	e
1.	0 ×9 = 0	3 ×6 = 18	7 ×5 = 35	5 ×6 = 30	3 ×2 = 6
2.	7 ×4 = 28	3 ×3 = 9	1 ×9 = 9	2 ×7 = 14	0 ×6 = 0
3.	6 ×3 = 18	3 ×4 = 12	4 ×1 = 4	7 ×0 = 0	4 ×2 = 8
4.	1 ×3 = 3	4 ×4 = 16	3 ×6 = 18	4 ×5 = 20	1 ×5 = 5

Spectrum Multiplication
Grade 3

Chapter 1
Single Digit Multiplication

9

Page 10

Multiplying through 9 × 9

Multiply.

	a	b	c	d	e
1.	9 ×9 = 27	7 ×6 = 42	5 ×4 = 20	7 ×9 = 63	8 ×6 = 48
2.	4 ×3 = 12	8 ×5 = 40	4 ×9 = 36	3 ×0 = 0	5 ×7 = 35
3.	5 ×1 = 5	4 ×6 = 24	8 ×2 = 16	6 ×8 = 48	4 ×0 = 0
4.	3 ×1 = 3	6 ×4 = 24	9 ×2 = 18	3 ×4 = 12	6 ×3 = 18

Spectrum Multiplication
Grade 3

Chapter 1
Single Digit Multiplication

10

Spectrum Multiplication
Grade 3

Answer Key

Answer Key

11 — Multiplying through 9 × 9

	a	b	c	d	e
1.	5 ×0 = 0	2 ×9 = 18	0 ×9 = 0	5 ×6 = 30	3 ×8 = 24
2.	3 ×6 = 18	7 ×6 = 42	9 ×9 = 81	8 ×4 = 32	5 ×3 = 15
3.	2 ×6 = 12	8 ×8 = 64	9 ×3 = 27	7 ×4 = 28	8 ×0 = 0
4.	7 ×7 = 49	3 ×7 = 21	8 ×9 = 72	5 ×5 = 25	9 ×1 = 9

12 — Single Digit Multiplication

	a	b	c	d	e
1.	3 ×3 = 9	8 ×7 = 56	2 ×9 = 18	7 ×5 = 35	9 ×4 = 36
2.	9 ×9 = 81	4 ×3 = 12	5 ×3 = 15	4 ×4 = 16	7 ×7 = 49
3.	8 ×5 = 40	6 ×4 = 24	8 ×2 = 16	9 ×7 = 63	4 ×8 = 32
4.	1 ×1 = 1	9 ×5 = 45	8 ×6 = 48	7 ×6 = 42	9 ×6 = 54

13 — Single Digit Multiplication

	a	b	c	d	e
1.	6 ×6 = 36	7 ×1 = 7	5 ×0 = 0	9 ×3 = 27	2 ×2 = 4
2.	3 ×3 = 9	7 ×3 = 21	5 ×5 = 25	9 ×8 = 72	7 ×8 = 56
3.	3 ×7 = 21	7 ×4 = 28	6 ×3 = 18	7 ×0 = 0	4 ×9 = 36
4.	6 ×5 = 30	7 ×2 = 14	9 ×1 = 9	3 ×9 = 27	6 ×8 = 48

14 — Single Digit Multiplication

	a	b	c	d	e
1.	7 ×2 = 14	2 ×9 = 18	2 ×5 = 10	6 ×2 = 12	5 ×2 = 10
2.	8 ×2 = 16	2 ×4 = 8	2 ×6 = 12	2 ×1 = 2	9 ×2 = 18
3.	2 ×2 = 4	2 ×3 = 6	4 ×2 = 8	2 ×8 = 16	1 ×2 = 2
4.	2 ×0 = 0	2 ×7 = 14	3 ×2 = 6	2 ×1 = 2	0 ×2 = 0

15 — Single Digit Multiplication (SCORE / 24)

	a	b	c	d	e
1.	5 ×3 = 15	9 ×3 = 27	3 ×7 = 21	5 ×3 = 15	3 ×3 = 9
2.	8 ×3 = 24	6 ×3 = 18	3 ×1 = 3	7 ×3 = 21	3 ×2 = 6
3.	3 ×5 = 15	3 ×4 = 12	3 ×9 = 27	3 ×5 = 15	0 ×3 = 0

Complete each table.

4.
a. Rule: multiply by 3

In	Out
2	6
4	12
6	18
8	24

b. Rule: multiply by 5

In	Out
5	25
3	15
7	35
9	45

c. Rule: multiply by 7

In	Out
4	28
8	56
9	63
7	49

16 — Single Digit Multiplication

Fill in the missing number.

	a	b	c	d	e
1.	6 ×[9] = 54	[7] × 6 = 42	5 ×[5] = 25	[1] × 5 = 5	8 ×[9] = 72
2.	4 ×[4] = 16	[2] × 4 = 8	[3] × 5 = 15	[7] × 7 = 49	[3] × 2 = 6
3.	[8] × 7 = 56	8 ×[3] = 24	[8] × 3 = 24	9 ×[7] = 63	[5] × 6 = 30
4.	3 ×[5] = 15	[8] × 8 = 64	4 ×[8] = 32	[9] × 5 = 45	[1] × 8 = 8

Page 17

Single Digit Multiplication

Multiply.

	a	b	c	d	e
1.	$6 \times 4 = 24$	$9 \times 4 = 36$	$4 \times 7 = 28$	$5 \times 4 = 20$	$4 \times 4 = 16$
2.	$8 \times 4 = 32$	$4 \times 6 = 24$	$4 \times 1 = 4$	$7 \times 4 = 28$	$4 \times 2 = 8$
3.	$4 \times 1 = 4$	$3 \times 4 = 12$	$4 \times 9 = 36$	$4 \times 5 = 20$	$0 \times 4 = 0$
4.	$4 \times 3 = 12$	$4 \times 8 = 32$	$1 \times 4 = 4$	$2 \times 4 = 8$	$4 \times 7 = 28$

Spectrum Multiplication
Grade 3
Chapter 1 — Single Digit Multiplication — **17**

Page 18

Single Digit Multiplication

Multiply.

	a	b	c	d	e
1.	$5 \times 6 = 30$	$4 \times 5 = 20$	$2 \times 5 = 10$	$5 \times 9 = 45$	$5 \times 2 = 10$
2.	$1 \times 5 = 5$	$6 \times 5 = 30$	$7 \times 5 = 35$	$5 \times 5 = 25$	$5 \times 1 = 5$
3.	$5 \times 3 = 15$	$0 \times 5 = 0$	$5 \times 8 = 40$	$9 \times 5 = 45$	$5 \times 7 = 35$
4.	$8 \times 5 = 40$	$5 \times 1 = 5$	$0 \times 5 = 0$	$3 \times 5 = 15$	$5 \times 4 = 20$

Spectrum Multiplication
Grade 3
Chapter 1 — Single Digit Multiplication — **18**

Page 19

Single Digit Multiplication

Multiply.

	a	b	c	d	e
1.	$6 \times 5 = 30$	$9 \times 5 = 45$	$5 \times 7 = 35$	$5 \times 5 = 25$	$5 \times 4 = 20$
2.	$8 \times 5 = 40$	$5 \times 6 = 30$	$5 \times 1 = 5$	$7 \times 5 = 35$	$5 \times 2 = 10$
3.	$5 \times 1 = 5$	$3 \times 5 = 15$	$5 \times 9 = 45$	$4 \times 5 = 20$	$0 \times 5 = 0$

Complete each table.

4.

a. Rule: multiply by 4

In	Out
5	20
1	4
8	32
7	28

b. Rule: multiply by 2

In	Out
9	18
2	4
6	12
3	6

c. Rule: multiply by 6

In	Out
8	48
4	24
6	36
1	6

Spectrum Multiplication
Grade 3
Chapter 1 — Single Digit Multiplication — **19**

Page 20

Single Digit Multiplication

Multiply.

	a	b	c	d	e
1.	$0 \times 6 = 0$	$2 \times 6 = 12$	$6 \times 6 = 36$	$6 \times 9 = 54$	$7 \times 6 = 42$
2.	$1 \times 6 = 6$	$9 \times 6 = 54$	$6 \times 1 = 6$	$6 \times 4 = 24$	$6 \times 1 = 6$
3.	$6 \times 7 = 42$	$4 \times 6 = 24$	$5 \times 6 = 30$	$8 \times 6 = 48$	$3 \times 6 = 18$
4.	$6 \times 0 = 0$	$6 \times 3 = 18$	$1 \times 6 = 6$	$6 \times 2 = 12$	$6 \times 5 = 30$

Spectrum Multiplication
Grade 3
Chapter 1 — Single Digit Multiplication — **20**

Page 21

Single Digit Multiplication

Fill in the missing number.

	a	b	c	d	e
1.	$9 \times 2 = 18$	$3 \times 4 = 12$	$8 \times 5 = 40$	$5 \times 6 = 30$	$6 \times 8 = 48$
2.	$7 \times 3 = 21$	$1 \times 2 = 2$	$7 \times 5 = 35$	$3 \times 5 = 15$	$8 \times 2 = 16$
3.	$6 \times 2 = 12$	$4 \times 6 = 24$	$7 \times 4 = 28$	$3 \times 9 = 27$	$1 \times 5 = 5$
4.	$4 \times 4 = 16$	$6 \times 6 = 36$	$6 \times 1 = 6$	$8 \times 3 = 24$	$5 \times 5 = 25$

Spectrum Multiplication
Grade 3
Chapter 1 — Single Digit Multiplication — **21**

Page 22

Single Digit Multiplication

Multiply.

	a	b	c	d	e
1.	$5 \times 7 = 35$	$7 \times 8 = 56$	$6 \times 7 = 42$	$7 \times 0 = 0$	$9 \times 7 = 63$
2.	$7 \times 7 = 49$	$7 \times 1 = 7$	$7 \times 4 = 28$	$7 \times 2 = 14$	$2 \times 7 = 14$
3.	$7 \times 1 = 7$	$2 \times 7 = 14$	$8 \times 7 = 56$	$7 \times 6 = 42$	$3 \times 7 = 21$
4.	$0 \times 7 = 0$	$7 \times 5 = 35$	$4 \times 7 = 28$	$1 \times 7 = 7$	$7 \times 9 = 63$

Spectrum Multiplication
Grade 3
Chapter 1 — Single Digit Multiplication — **22**

Answer Key

Page 23

Single Digit Multiplication

Multiply.

	a	b	c	d	e
1.	6 ×5 = 30	1 ×7 = 7	0 ×6 = 0	8 ×2 = 16	7 ×8 = 56
2.	4 ×5 = 20	3 ×0 = 0	7 ×4 = 28	4 ×9 = 36	3 ×6 = 18
3.	7 ×2 = 14	9 ×7 = 63	2 ×4 = 8	5 ×7 = 35	2 ×5 = 10

Complete each table.

4.

a) Rule: multiply by 8

In	Out
5	40
4	32
3	24
2	16

b) Rule: multiply by 7

In	Out
2	14
7	49
5	35
8	56

c) Rule: multiply by 1

In	Out
3	3
5	5
7	7
9	9

23

Page 24

Single Digit Multiplication

Multiply.

	a	b	c	d	e
1.	8 ×9 = 72	1 ×8 = 8	4 ×8 = 32	8 ×5 = 40	0 ×8 = 0
2.	3 ×8 = 24	8 ×6 = 48	2 ×8 = 16	8 ×7 = 56	8 ×1 = 8
3.	2 ×8 = 16	8 ×4 = 32	8 ×2 = 16	8 ×1 = 8	8 ×8 = 64
4.	9 ×8 = 72	8 ×0 = 0	6 ×8 = 48	5 ×8 = 40	8 ×3 = 24

24

Page 25

Single Digit Multiplication

Fill in the missing number.

	a	b	c	d	e
1.	[8] ×8 = 64	8 ×5 = 40	6 ×8 = 48	3 ×8 = 24	1 ×8 = 8
2.	4 ×8 = 32	[8] ×9 = 72	1 ×[8] = 8	5 ×8 = 40	8 ×3 = 24
3.	[8] ×2 = 16	[8] ×7 = 56	8 ×6 = [48]	2 ×8 = [16]	[5] ×8 = 40
4.	6 ×8 = [48]	8 ×[4] = 32	9 ×8 = [72]	8 ×3 = [24]	8 ×0 = [0]

25

Page 26

Single Digit Multiplication

Multiply.

	a	b	c	d	e
1.	9 ×7 = 63	3 ×9 = 27	9 ×8 = 72	9 ×6 = 54	4 ×9 = 36
2.	9 ×3 = 27	9 ×1 = 9	5 ×9 = 45	9 ×9 = 81	2 ×9 = 18
3.	9 ×7 = 63	9 ×4 = 36	8 ×9 = 72	9 ×2 = 18	9 ×5 = 45
4.	0 ×9 = 0	9 ×3 = 27	6 ×9 = 54	9 ×9 = 81	9 ×1 = 9

26

Page 27

Single Digit Multiplication

Multiply.

	a	b	c	d	e
1.	0 ×8 = 0	2 ×5 = 10	1 ×6 = 6	5 ×8 = 40	7 ×6 = 42
2.	5 ×6 = 30	3 ×8 = 24	9 ×6 = 54	5 ×7 = 35	6 ×5 = 30
3.	7 ×5 = 35	2 ×8 = 16	1 ×7 = 7	5 ×0 = 0	4 ×7 = 28

Complete each table.

4.

a) Rule: multiply by 9

In	Out
8	72
7	63
6	54
5	45

b) Rule: multiply by 2

In	Out
2	4
4	8
6	12
8	16

c) Rule: multiply by 5

In	Out
4	20
7	35
3	15
9	45

27

Page 28

Single Digit Multiplication

Multiply.

	a	b	c	d	e
1.	0 ×7 = 0	4 ×3 = 12	1 ×5 = 5	2 ×6 = 12	4 ×7 = 28
2.	4 ×8 = 32	3 ×6 = 18	5 ×5 = 25	9 ×6 = 54	4 ×2 = 8
3.	2 ×5 = 10	6 ×6 = 36	1 ×4 = 4	4 ×5 = 20	8 ×6 = 48
4.	6 ×5 = 30	7 ×3 = 21	4 ×4 = 16	4 ×6 = 24	7 ×9 = 63

28

Answer Key

Answer Key

Page 29

NAME _____ SCORE ⬤ / 16

Number Sentences

A **number sentence** is an equation with numbers.

Identity Property
for multiplication: 1 × 3 = 3

Commutative Property
for multiplication: 4 × 2 = 2 × 4

A number sentence can change its look but not change its value.

3 × 8 = 24 or 3 × 8 = 6 × 4

Complete each number sentence.

	a	b	c	d
1.	1 × 2 = [2]	1 × 5 = [5]	[1] × 4 = 4	[1] × 9 = 9
2.	5 × 7 = 7 × [5]	4 × [3] = 3 × 4	[5] × 3 = 3 × 5	9 × 4 = [4] × 9

Complete the following.

	a	b	c	d
3.	5 × 6 = 30 or	4 × 3 = 12 or	6 × 3 = 18 or	6 × 2 = 12 or
	5 × 6 = 10 × [3]	4 × 3 = 2 × [6]	6 × 3 = 9 × [2]	6 × 2 = 4 × [3]
4.	8 × 5 = 40 or	4 × 4 = 16 or	9 × 4 = 36 or	2 × 10 = 20 or
	8 × 5 = 4 × [10]	4 × 4 = 2 × [8]	9 × 4 = 6 × [6]	2 × 10 = 4 × [5]

Spectrum Multiplication
Grade 3

Chapter 1
Single Digit Multiplication
29

29

Page 30

NAME _____ SCORE ⬤ / 24

Single Digit Multiplication

Complete the following.

	a		b	
1.	7 × 3 = [21]		6 × 5 = [30]	
	3 × 7 = [21]		5 × 6 = [30]	
2.	2 × 3 = [6]		4 × 6 = [24]	
	3 × 2 = [6]		6 × 4 = [24]	
3.	2 × 9 = [18]		8 × 4 = [32]	
	9 × 2 = [18]		4 × 8 = [32]	
4.	7 × 2 = [14]		3 × 6 = [18]	
	2 × 7 = [14]		6 × 3 = [18]	
5.	9 × 4 = [36]		8 × 3 = [24]	
	4 × 9 = [36]		3 × 8 = [24]	
6.	5 × 2 = [10]		9 × 3 = [27]	
	2 × 5 = [10]		3 × 9 = [27]	

Spectrum Multiplication
Grade 3

Chapter 1
Single Digit Multiplication
30

30

Page 31

NAME _____

💡 **Check What You Learned**

Single Digit Multiplication

Multiply.

	a	b	c	d	e
1.	3 ×6 = 18	8 ×2 = 16	4 ×9 = 36	7 ×9 = 42	6 ×6 = 36
2.	7 ×7 = 49	5 ×5 = 25	4 ×3 = 12	6 ×8 = 48	7 ×4 = 28
3.	5 ×9 = 45	9 ×8 = 72	5 ×6 = 30	4 ×2 = 8	6 ×3 = 18
4.	5 ×5 = 20	7 ×2 = 14	6 ×5 = 30	8 ×6 = 48	7 ×8 = 56
5.	8 ×5 = 40	9 ×7 = 63	7 ×3 = 21	4 ×6 = 24	8 ×9 = 72

Fill in the missing numbers.

	a	b	c	d	e
6.	[8] × 8 = 64	6 × [7] = 42	[6] × 9 = 54	[4] × 4 = 16	5 × [3] = 15

Spectrum Multiplication
Grade 3

Chapter 1
Single Digit Multiplication
31

31

Page 32

NAME _____

🔍 **Check What You Know**

Problem Solving: Single Digit Multiplication

Read the problem carefully and solve. Show your work under each question.

Kevin buys school supplies. He buys markers, pencils, pens, and erasers.

1. Pencils come in packages of 6. If Kevin buys 4 packages, how many pencils will he have?

   ___24___ pencils

2. Markers come in packages of 7. If Kevin buys 5 packages, how many markers will he have?

   ___35___ markers

3. Erasers come in boxes of 9. If Kevin buys 8 boxes and gives 3 boxes to his little brother, how many erasers will he have?

   ___45___ erasers

4. Pens come in packages of 8. Kevin wants to know how many pens he will have if he buys 3 packages. How can he write and solve this as an addition problem?

   ___8 + 8 + 8 = 24___ pens

Spectrum Multiplication
Grade 3

Chapter 2
Problem Solving: Single Digit Multiplication
32

32

Page 33

NAME _____ SCORE ⬤ / 3

Understanding Multiplication

Read the problem carefully and solve. Show your work under each question.

Dylan makes fruit baskets to give to his family. In each basket, Dylan puts in 3 pears, 5 bananas, and 6 apples.

> **Helpful Hint**
> When multiplying, remember that multiplication can be written and solved as an addition problem.
> Examples:
> 6 × 2 means the same as 6 + 6
> 4 × 3 means the same as 4 + 4 + 4

1. Dylan wrote down 5 × 2 to find out how many bananas he will need to make 2 fruit baskets. Write and solve the corresponding addition problem.

   ___5 + 5 = 10___

2. Dylan wrote down 3 × 3 to find out how many pears he will need to make 3 fruit baskets. Write and solve the corresponding addition problem.

   ___3 + 3 + 3 = 9___

3. Dylan wants to know how many apples he will need to make 3 fruit baskets. What multiplication problem should Dylan write to find the answer? Solve the problem.

   ___6 × 3 = 18___

Spectrum Multiplication
Grade 3

Chapter 2
Problem Solving: Single Digit Multiplication
33

33

Page 34

NAME _____ SCORE ⬤ / 3

Multiplying through 5 × 9

Read the problem carefully and solve. Show your work under each question.

Emilio and Maria each make a photo album. Maria can fit 3 photos on each page of her album. She fills 9 pages. Emilio can fit 4 photos on each page of his album. He fills 7 pages.

> **Helpful Hint**
> To solve a multiplication word problem, you need to find:
> 1. the number of groups
> 2. the number of items in each group

1. Who has the most photos in their album, Emilio or Maria?

   ___Emilio___ has the most photos.

2. Maria takes all the photos from 3 pages of her album to school. How many photos does she take to school?

   ___9___ photos

3. Emilio adds some photos to his album. He fills 2 more pages. How many photos does Emilio have in his album now?

   ___36___ photos

Spectrum Multiplication
Grade 3

Chapter 2
Problem Solving: Single Digit Multiplication
34

34

Answer Key

Page 35

NAME _____   SCORE ⬤/4

Single Digit Multiplication

Read the problem carefully and solve. Show your work under each question.

Ella makes necklaces for a craft fair. For each necklace, she uses 4 yellow beads, 7 blue beads, 6 red beads, and 8 green beads.

Helpful Hint
If you know the total number of items in a group and the number of groups, then you can write an equation to help you solve the problem using multiplication:
$3 \times a = 18$
$3 \times 6 = 18$
$a = 6$

1. Ella finds 72 green beads in her backpack. She plans to make 9 necklaces with the 72 beads. Write a multiplication equation to find how many beads Ella will use on each necklace. Then, solve.

$9 \times a = 72$

_____8_____ beads

2. Ella wants to make 8 more necklaces. How many more blue beads will she need? How many more green beads will she need?

_____56_____ blue beads

_____64_____ green beads

Spectrum Multiplication
Grade 3
Problem Solving: Single Digit Multiplication   Chapter 2
35

35

Page 36

NAME _____   SCORE ⬤/6

Single Digit Multiplication

Read the problem carefully and solve. Show your work under each question.

Ella makes necklaces for a craft fair. For each necklace, she uses 4 yellow beads, 7 blue beads, 6 red beads, and 8 green beads.

1. To make 6 necklaces, how many red beads does Ella use?

_____36_____ red beads

2. Ella wants to make 5 extra necklaces for her friends. But, she is out of yellow beads. How many yellow beads will she need to buy to make the necklaces?

_____20_____ yellow beads

3. Ella's necklaces are a big hit. She needs to make 7 more during the craft fair. How many more beads in each color will she need?

_____28_____ yellow beads

_____49_____ blue beads

_____42_____ red beads

_____56_____ green beads

Spectrum Multiplication
Grade 3
36
Problem Solving: Single Digit Multiplication   Chapter 2

36

Page 37

NAME _____   SCORE ⬤/6

Single Digit Multiplication

Solve each problem. Show your work under each question.

1. Steven wants to buy 6 pieces of bubblegum. Each piece costs 5 cents. How much will he have to pay for the bubblegum?

Steven wants to buy _____6_____ pieces of bubblegum.

One piece of bubblegum costs _____5_____ cents.

Steven will have to pay _____30_____ cents total.

2. There are 7 girls on stage. Each girl is holding 9 flowers. How many flowers are there in all?

There are _____7_____ girls.

Each girl is holding _____9_____ flowers.

There are _____63_____ flowers in all.

Spectrum Multiplication
Grade 3
Problem Solving: Single Digit Multiplication   Chapter 2
37

37

Page 38

NAME _____   SCORE ⬤/5

Single Digit Multiplication

Solve each problem. Show your work under each question.

1. There are 4 rows of desks. There are 8 desks in each row. How many desks are there in all?

There are _____4_____ rows of desks.

There are _____8_____ desks in each row.

There are _____32_____ desks in all.

2. Sara earns 4 dollars a day babysitting her cousin. If Sara babysits for 5 days two weeks in a row, how much money will she earn?

Sara will earn _____40_____ dollars.

3. Jose scored 16 total points during a basketball game. He scored the same number of points in each of the 4 quarters. Write a multiplication equation to find how many points he scored each quarter. Then, solve.

$4 \times a = 16$

He scored _____4_____ points each quarter.

Spectrum Multiplication
Grade 3
38
Problem Solving: Single Digit Multiplication   Chapter 2

38

Page 39

NAME _____   SCORE ⬤/3

Number Sentences

Read the problem carefully and solve. Show your work under each question.

Mr. Glenn splits his students into pairs. Each pair of students has to count the number of crayons they brought to class. Next, they will write a number sentence that compares the number of crayons they brought to class.

1. Helen organized her crayons into 3 groups of 7 crayons. She then organized her crayons into 7 equal groups. Complete the number sentence to find out how many crayons are in each of the 7 groups.

$3 \times 7 = 7 \times \boxed{3}$

2. Maria brought 4 groups of 2 crayons to class. Fred reorganized Maria's crayons into 2 equal groups of crayons. Complete the number sentence to show how many crayons are in the two groups.

$4 \times 2 = 2 \times \boxed{4}$

3. Greg put 1 crayon into 6 different groups. Complete the number sentence to find out how many crayons Gregg has total.

$6 \times 1 = \boxed{6}$

Spectrum Multiplication
Grade 3
Problem Solving: Single Digit Multiplication   Chapter 2
39

39

Page 40

NAME _____

💡 **Check What You Learned**

Problem Solving: Single Digit Multiplication

Read the problem carefully and solve. Show your work under each question.

The students at P.S. 134 are having a book sale. They are arranging the books into categories and stacking them on tables.

1. Josh sorted books about sports. When he was finished, he had 8 stacks of 6 books each. Kate brought over 6 more stacks with 8 books each. How many sports books in all were at the sale?

_____64_____ sports books

2. The largest category of books was fiction. Rebecca had 2 stacks with 8 books in each stack. How many fiction books were at the sale?

_____16_____ fiction books

3. The book sale was in the gym. The students set up tables into 9 rows with 4 tables in each row. What was the total number of tables in the gym?

_____36_____ tables

4. The customers were excited by the sale. They lined up to pay for their books. There were 5 lines with 7 customers in each line. How many customers were waiting to pay?

_____35_____ customers

Spectrum Multiplication
Grade 3
40
Problem Solving: Single Digit Multiplication   Chapter 2

40

Spectrum Multiplication
Grade 3

Answer Key

Answer Key

Mid-Test Chapters 1–2

Fill in the missing number.

	a	b	c	d	e
1.	7 ×[2] = 14	9 ×7 = 63	[2] ×4 = 8	5 ×7 = 35	[2] ×5 = 10
2.	[6] ×6 = 36	8 ×5 = 40	5 ×[5] = 25	6 ×[8] = 48	9 ×4 = 36
3.	3 ×[6] = 18	[4] ×9 = 36	7 ×4 = [28]	3 ×[1] = 3	4 ×5 = 20
4.	7 ×8 = [56]	8 ×[2] = 16	[1] ×6 = 6	[1] ×7 = 7	6 ×5 = [30]

Spectrum Multiplication
Grade 3

Mid-Test
Chapters 1–2
41

41

Mid-Test Chapters 1–2

Multiply.

	a	b	c	d	e
5.	4 ×9 = 36	3 ×4 = 12	3 ×7 = 21	2 ×5 = 10	2 ×4 = 8
6.	4 ×8 = 32	2 ×0 = 0	3 ×2 = 6	2 ×8 = 16	4 ×7 = 28
7.	2 ×6 = 12	3 ×1 = 3	4 ×1 = 4	4 ×6 = 24	2 ×4 = 8

Complete each table.

a Rule: multiply by 5		b Rule: multiply by 3		c Rule: multiply by 6	
In	Out	In	Out	In	Out
9	45	0	0	6	36
4	20	7	21	3	18
1	5	2	6	1	6
8	40	8	24	9	54

Spectrum Multiplication
Grade 3
42

Mid-Test
Chapters 1–2

42

Mid-Test Chapters 1–2

Read the problem carefully and solve. Show your work under each question.

The students at Kyle's school are having a bake sale. Kyle and his friends arrange the baked goods on the tables according to category.

9. At the cookie table, there are 2 lines with 9 customers in each line. How many customers were waiting to buy cookies?

_____18_____ customers

10. Ming sorted 56 brownies into stacks. She made 8 stacks with the same number of brownies in each stack. Write a multiplication equation to find how many brownies are in each stack. Then, solve.

8 × a = 56

_____7_____ brownies

11. Kyle was selling cakes for $5 each. Kyle's teacher bought 5 cakes for a party. How much did the teacher pay for the cakes?

_____25_____ dollars

12. When the sale was over, the students counted the money. Bruno counted 5 five-dollar bills. Leo counted 4 five-dollar bills. How much money did they count altogether?

_____45_____ dollars

Spectrum Multiplication
Grade 3

Mid-Test
Chapters 1–2
43

43

Check What You Know

Multiplying 2 Digits by 1 Digit

Multiply.

	a	b	c	d	e
1.	26 ×3 = 78	24 ×4 = 96	47 ×2 = 94	14 ×6 = 84	53 ×4 = 212
2.	39 ×2 = 78	14 ×7 = 98	25 ×3 = 75	13 ×5 = 65	37 ×2 = 74
3.	48 ×2 = 96	23 ×4 = 92	35 ×2 = 70	12 ×8 = 96	24 ×3 = 72
4.	13 ×6 = 78	18 ×5 = 90	29 ×3 = 87	17 ×5 = 85	49 ×2 = 98
5.	16 ×6 = 96	36 ×2 = 72	18 ×3 = 54	15 ×6 = 90	27 ×3 = 81
6.	13 ×7 = 91	28 ×3 = 84	19 ×5 = 95	46 ×2 = 92	16 ×5 = 80

Spectrum Multiplication
Grade 3

Chapter 3
Multiplying 2 Digits by 1 Digit
44

44

SCORE ___ / 20

Multiplying 2 Digits by 1 Digit

Multiply 2 ones by 3.	Multiply 8 tens by 3.		
82 ×3 = 6	82 ×3 = 6	82 ×3 = 6 +240	82 ×3 = 6 +240 = 246 > factor factor Add. product

Multiply. Show your work.

	a	b	c	d	e
1.	73 ×2 = 6 +140 = 146	14 ×2 = 8 +20 = 28	90 ×5 = 0 +450 = 450	45 ×1 = 5 +40 = 45	33 ×3 = 9 +90 = 99
2.	22 ×4 = 8 +80 = 88	86 ×1 = 6 +80 = 86	52 ×4 = 8 +200 = 208	31 ×5 = 5 +150 = 155	46 ×1 = 6 +40 = 46
3.	19 ×1 = 9 +10 = 19	21 ×4 = 4 +80 = 84	43 ×3 = 9 +120 = 129	27 ×1 = 7 +20 = 27	91 ×5 = 5 +450 = 455
4.	56 ×1 = 6 +50 = 56	52 ×2 = 4 +100 = 104	63 ×3 = 9 +180 = 189	73 ×1 = 3 +70 = 73	62 ×2 = 4 +120 = 124

Spectrum Multiplication
Grade 3

Chapter 3
Multiplying 2 Digits by 1 Digit
45

45

SCORE ___ / 20

Multiplication and Place Value

Use place value to multiply by multiples of 10.

9 × 40 = 9 ones × 4 tens   Multiply 9 ones by 4 tens.

9 × 4 tens = 36 tens = 360

9 × 40 = 360

Multiply.

	a	b	c	d	e
1.	10 ×4 = 40	20 ×6 = 120	40 ×2 = 80	50 ×9 = 450	40 ×6 = 240
2.	80 ×9 = 720	60 ×3 = 180	30 ×8 = 240	90 ×2 = 180	70 ×3 = 210
3.	50 ×4 = 200	80 ×5 = 400	60 ×7 = 420	90 ×3 = 270	20 ×5 = 100
4.	60 ×6 = 360	70 ×2 = 140	80 ×8 = 640	40 ×5 = 200	50 ×6 = 300

Spectrum Multiplication
Grade 3
46

Chapter 3
Multiplying 2 Digits by 1 Digit

46

Answer Key

47

NAME _____ SCORE ◯ / 25

Multiplication and Place Value

Multiply.

	a	b	c	d	e
1.	50 ×6 = 300	70 ×3 = 210	80 ×5 = 400	60 ×7 = 420	30 ×4 = 120
2.	90 ×9 = 810	50 ×3 = 150	60 ×8 = 480	10 ×8 = 80	20 ×3 = 60
3.	20 ×4 = 80	10 ×5 = 50	90 ×8 = 720	30 ×7 = 210	60 ×5 = 300
4.	10 ×9 = 90	30 ×8 = 240	40 ×7 = 280	60 ×7 = 420	40 ×7 = 280
5.	80 ×8 = 640	90 ×6 = 540	30 ×3 = 90	70 ×4 = 280	10 ×6 = 60

Spectrum Multiplication
Grade 3
Chapter 3 — Multiplying 2 Digits by 1 Digit — 47

48

NAME _____ SCORE ◯ / 25

Multiplication Practice

Multiply.

	a	b	c	d	e
1.	23 ×2 = 46	71 ×1 = 71	12 ×4 = 48	33 ×2 = 66	10 ×7 = 70
2.	44 ×2 = 88	43 ×2 = 86	90 ×1 = 90	22 ×4 = 88	12 ×3 = 36
3.	11 ×9 = 99	75 ×1 = 75	11 ×6 = 66	30 ×3 = 90	10 ×4 = 40
4.	11 ×7 = 77	10 ×2 = 20	33 ×0 = 0	13 ×3 = 39	20 ×3 = 60
5.	10 ×2 = 20	41 ×2 = 82	13 ×2 = 26	40 ×2 = 80	30 ×2 = 60

Spectrum Multiplication
Grade 3
Chapter 3 — Multiplying 2 Digits by 1 Digit — 48

49

NAME _____ SCORE ◯ / 25

Multiplication Practice

Multiply.

	a	b	c	d	e
1.	24 ×2 = 48	14 ×2 = 28	42 ×2 = 84	31 ×2 = 62	11 ×5 = 55
2.	30 ×1 = 30	11 ×7 = 77	25 ×1 = 25	42 ×0 = 0	22 ×3 = 66
3.	10 ×1 = 10	14 ×0 = 0	10 ×5 = 50	31 ×3 = 93	12 ×3 = 36
4.	20 ×4 = 80	10 ×7 = 70	15 ×1 = 15	20 ×3 = 60	11 ×3 = 33
5.	60 ×1 = 60	43 ×2 = 86	33 ×3 = 99	11 ×9 = 99	28 ×0 = 0

Spectrum Multiplication
Grade 3
Chapter 3 — Multiplying 2 Digits by 1 Digit — 49

50

NAME _____ SCORE ◯ / 25

Multiplication Practice

Multiply.

	a	b	c	d	e
1.	32 ×3 = 96	21 ×4 = 84	33 ×2 = 66	30 ×3 = 90	21 ×2 = 42
2.	43 ×2 = 86	20 ×3 = 60	11 ×4 = 44	34 ×2 = 68	21 ×3 = 63
3.	33 ×3 = 99	24 ×2 = 48	22 ×4 = 88	40 ×2 = 80	32 ×2 = 64
4.	13 ×3 = 39	22 ×2 = 44	20 ×4 = 80	23 ×2 = 46	11 ×3 = 33
5.	41 ×2 = 82	31 ×3 = 93	44 ×2 = 88	23 ×3 = 69	12 ×4 = 48

Spectrum Multiplication
Grade 3
Chapter 3 — Multiplying 2 Digits by 1 Digit — 50

51

NAME _____ SCORE ◯ / 15

Multiplying 2 Digits by 1 Digit (with renaming)

Multiply 6 ones by 3.

26 × 3, 3 × 6 = 18 = 10 + 8

Multiply 2 tens by 3. Add the 1 ten.

3 × 20 = 60, 60 + 10 = 70

26 ◄ factor
× 3 ◄ factor
78 ◄ product

Multiply.

	a	b	c	d	e
1.	37 ×2 = 74	19 ×5 = 95	45 ×2 = 90	38 ×2 = 76	25 ×3 = 75
2.	14 ×4 = 56	47 ×2 = 94	28 ×3 = 84	13 ×4 = 52	23 ×4 = 92
3.	26 ×2 = 52	36 ×2 = 72	13 ×5 = 65	15 ×3 = 45	27 ×2 = 54

Spectrum Multiplication
Grade 3
Chapter 3 — Multiplying 2 Digits by 1 Digit — 51

52

NAME _____ SCORE ◯ / 25

Multiplying 2 Digits by 1 Digit (with renaming)

Multiply.

	a	b	c	d	e
1.	12 ×5 = 60	24 ×4 = 96	18 ×5 = 90	15 ×5 = 75	17 ×3 = 51
2.	24 ×3 = 72	39 ×2 = 78	14 ×5 = 70	16 ×2 = 32	27 ×3 = 81
3.	15 ×4 = 60	29 ×2 = 58	26 ×3 = 78	36 ×2 = 72	17 ×5 = 85
4.	35 ×2 = 70	25 ×2 = 50	28 ×2 = 56	14 ×3 = 42	17 ×4 = 68
5.	29 ×3 = 87	19 ×3 = 57	23 ×4 = 92	38 ×2 = 76	13 ×6 = 78

Spectrum Multiplication
Grade 3
Chapter 3 — Multiplying 2 Digits by 1 Digit — 52

Answer Key

53

NAME
Multiplication Practice — SCORE /20

Multiply.

	a	b	c	d	e
1.	72 × 5 = 360	38 × 4 = 152	29 × 5 = 145	27 × 4 = 108	25 × 5 = 125
2.	54 × 3 = 162	96 × 3 = 288	84 × 4 = 336	92 × 5 = 460	47 × 3 = 141
3.	45 × 3 = 135	23 × 5 = 115	86 × 3 = 258	73 × 5 = 365	22 × 5 = 110
4.	64 × 3 = 192	93 × 4 = 372	86 × 5 = 430	43 × 4 = 172	38 × 3 = 114

Spectrum Multiplication — Grade 3 — Chapter 3 — Multiplying 2 Digits by 1 Digit

54

Multiplication Practice — SCORE /20

Multiply.

	a	b	c	d	e
1.	36 × 4 = 144	86 × 2 = 172	56 × 4 = 224	74 × 4 = 296	34 × 3 = 102
2.	28 × 5 = 140	37 × 3 = 111	46 × 4 = 184	23 × 5 = 115	83 × 4 = 332
3.	44 × 3 = 132	59 × 3 = 177	82 × 5 = 410	74 × 5 = 370	63 × 4 = 252
4.	47 × 4 = 188	85 × 3 = 255	37 × 6 = 222	19 × 9 = 171	84 × 5 = 420

Spectrum Multiplication — Grade 3 — Chapter 3 — Multiplying 2 Digits by 1 Digit

55

Multiplication Practice — SCORE /25

Multiply.

	a	b	c	d	e
1.	73 × 4 = 292	25 × 2 = 50	36 × 3 = 108	52 × 5 = 260	23 × 4 = 92
2.	19 × 2 = 38	26 × 2 = 52	68 × 3 = 204	54 × 5 = 270	47 × 8 = 376
3.	32 × 9 = 288	48 × 8 = 384	52 × 3 = 156	34 × 4 = 136	17 × 5 = 85
4.	66 × 3 = 198	45 × 5 = 225	66 × 5 = 330	19 × 9 = 171	38 × 9 = 342
5.	55 × 3 = 165	64 × 8 = 512	83 × 5 = 415	49 × 7 = 343	50 × 9 = 450

Spectrum Multiplication — Grade 3 — Chapter 3 — Multiplying 2 Digits by 1 Digit

56

Multiplication Practice — SCORE /25

Multiply.

	a	b	c	d	e
1.	42 × 5 = 210	33 × 4 = 132	22 × 5 = 110	74 × 3 = 222	86 × 6 = 516
2.	60 × 6 = 360	17 × 3 = 51	48 × 9 = 432	75 × 3 = 225	60 × 9 = 540
3.	96 × 5 = 480	31 × 9 = 279	77 × 4 = 308	82 × 3 = 246	96 × 3 = 288
4.	40 × 7 = 280	79 × 2 = 158	52 × 5 = 260	46 × 3 = 138	27 × 8 = 216
5.	39 × 6 = 234	43 × 7 = 301	83 × 2 = 166	24 × 8 = 192	55 × 3 = 165

Spectrum Multiplication — Grade 3 — Chapter 3 — Multiplying 2 Digits by 1 Digit

57

Multiplication Practice — SCORE /20

Multiply.

	a	b	c	d	e
1.	16 × 3 = 48	28 × 2 = 56	34 × 7 = 238	22 × 9 = 198	17 × 6 = 102
2.	74 × 6 = 444	34 × 9 = 306	28 × 6 = 168	63 × 1 = 63	17 × 4 = 68
3.	36 × 4 = 144	27 × 8 = 216	52 × 2 = 104	73 × 7 = 511	65 × 9 = 585
4.	26 × 5 = 130	84 × 8 = 672	92 × 3 = 276	58 × 4 = 232	36 × 8 = 288

Spectrum Multiplication — Grade 3 — Chapter 3 — Multiplying 2 Digits by 1 Digit

58

Multiplication Practice — SCORE /20

Multiply.

	a	b	c	d	e
1.	42 × 7 = 294	65 × 5 = 325	87 × 2 = 174	49 × 6 = 294	70 × 5 = 350
2.	46 × 7 = 322	28 × 9 = 252	37 × 2 = 74	97 × 1 = 97	52 × 4 = 208
3.	16 × 5 = 80	76 × 2 = 152	73 × 3 = 219	56 × 8 = 448	75 × 4 = 300
4.	93 × 6 = 558	28 × 3 = 84	45 × 4 = 180	18 × 6 = 108	12 × 9 = 108

Spectrum Multiplication — Grade 3 — Chapter 3 — Multiplying 2 Digits by 1 Digit

Answer Key

Answer Key

Page 59 — Multiplication Practice (SCORE __/20)

Multiply.

	a	b	c	d	e
1.	86 × 3 = 258	72 × 5 = 360	67 × 4 = 268	91 × 9 = 819	22 × 7 = 154
2.	51 × 2 = 102	38 × 7 = 266	43 × 8 = 344	29 × 1 = 29	18 × 6 = 108
3.	57 × 6 = 342	16 × 9 = 144	82 × 5 = 410	33 × 3 = 99	17 × 8 = 136
4.	13 × 6 = 78	10 × 7 = 70	73 × 5 = 365	64 × 8 = 512	31 × 9 = 279

Spectrum Multiplication, Grade 3 — Chapter 3, Multiplying 2 Digits by 1 Digit — 59

Page 60 — Multiplication Practice (SCORE __/20)

Multiply.

	a	b	c	d	e
1.	65 × 5 = 325	46 × 1 = 46	29 × 5 = 145	28 × 7 = 196	36 × 3 = 108
2.	84 × 3 = 252	69 × 7 = 483	16 × 5 = 80	44 × 2 = 88	39 × 1 = 39
3.	87 × 6 = 522	17 × 3 = 51	34 × 5 = 170	53 × 2 = 106	39 × 8 = 312
4.	15 × 4 = 60	62 × 3 = 186	19 × 3 = 57	22 × 4 = 88	23 × 4 = 92

Spectrum Multiplication, Grade 3 — Chapter 3, Multiplying 2 Digits by 1 Digit — 60

Page 61 — Multiplication Practice (SCORE __/25)

Multiply.

	a	b	c	d	e
1.	31 × 5 = 155	42 × 2 = 84	36 × 1 = 36	52 × 4 = 208	83 × 3 = 249
2.	39 × 1 = 39	41 × 4 = 164	52 × 2 = 104	28 × 1 = 28	13 × 3 = 39
3.	54 × 2 = 108	17 × 1 = 17	29 × 0 = 0	23 × 3 = 69	42 × 4 = 168
4.	61 × 5 = 305	72 × 3 = 216	14 × 2 = 28	86 × 1 = 86	47 × 1 = 47
5.	83 × 2 = 166	42 × 3 = 126	69 × 3 = 207	11 × 5 = 55	61 × 2 = 122

Spectrum Multiplication, Grade 3 — Chapter 3, Multiplying 2 Digits by 1 Digit — 61

Page 62 — Multiplication Practice (SCORE __/25)

Multiply.

	a	b	c	d	e
1.	75 × 1 = 75	30 × 5 = 150	41 × 5 = 205	92 × 3 = 276	58 × 1 = 58
2.	13 × 2 = 26	10 × 5 = 50	23 × 2 = 46	42 × 1 = 42	82 × 4 = 328
3.	31 × 4 = 124	22 × 3 = 66	33 × 2 = 66	43 × 3 = 129	52 × 3 = 156
4.	92 × 2 = 184	54 × 1 = 54	14 × 1 = 14	52 × 3 = 156	17 × 0 = 0
5.	34 × 2 = 68	30 × 4 = 120	65 × 1 = 65	23 × 2 = 46	11 × 4 = 44

Spectrum Multiplication, Grade 3 — Chapter 3, Multiplying 2 Digits by 1 Digit — 62

Page 63 — Multiplication Practice (SCORE __/25)

Multiply.

	a	b	c	d	e
1.	37 × 4 = 148	48 × 3 = 144	23 × 6 = 138	97 × 2 = 194	47 × 5 = 235
2.	76 × 2 = 152	59 × 4 = 236	34 × 6 = 204	38 × 5 = 190	48 × 2 = 96
3.	45 × 6 = 270	67 × 3 = 201	43 × 4 = 172	85 × 2 = 170	39 × 5 = 195
4.	64 × 3 = 192	83 × 6 = 498	45 × 3 = 135	63 × 5 = 315	93 × 4 = 372
5.	86 × 2 = 172	73 × 5 = 365	66 × 4 = 264	25 × 6 = 150	74 × 3 = 222

Spectrum Multiplication, Grade 3 — Chapter 3, Multiplying 2 Digits by 1 Digit — 63

Page 64 — Multiplication Practice (SCORE __/25)

Multiply.

	a	b	c	d	e
1.	13 × 5 = 65	38 × 2 = 76	48 × 2 = 96	19 × 4 = 76	29 × 3 = 87
2.	14 × 8 = 112	15 × 6 = 90	36 × 3 = 108	39 × 2 = 78	27 × 4 = 108
3.	28 × 3 = 84	47 × 2 = 94	16 × 9 = 144	15 × 5 = 75	13 × 7 = 91
4.	17 × 6 = 102	25 × 4 = 100	24 × 3 = 72	45 × 2 = 90	16 × 8 = 128
5.	14 × 7 = 98	29 × 2 = 58	16 × 4 = 64	37 × 3 = 111	16 × 5 = 80

Spectrum Multiplication, Grade 3 — Chapter 3, Multiplying 2 Digits by 1 Digit — 64

Answer Key

Answer Key

Page 65 — Multiplication Practice

	a	b	c	d	e
1.	26 × 3 = 78	64 × 5 = 320	65 × 5 = 325	34 × 8 = 272	47 × 6 = 282
2.	43 × 8 = 344	57 × 6 = 342	98 × 2 = 196	35 × 4 = 140	76 × 3 = 228
3.	46 × 7 = 322	85 × 3 = 255	35 × 8 = 280	23 × 9 = 207	62 × 5 = 310
4.	42 × 6 = 252	73 × 4 = 292	82 × 5 = 410	67 × 3 = 201	27 × 8 = 216
5.	49 × 7 = 343	88 × 2 = 176	36 × 9 = 324	53 × 6 = 318	83 × 4 = 332

Page 66 — Multiplication Practice

	a	b	c	d	e
1.	84 × 5 = 420	35 × 7 = 245	64 × 7 = 448	43 × 9 = 387	28 × 6 = 168
2.	63 × 8 = 504	57 × 4 = 228	55 × 9 = 495	43 × 6 = 258	92 × 8 = 736
3.	42 × 9 = 378	85 × 6 = 510	53 × 4 = 212	74 × 8 = 592	83 × 5 = 415
4.	65 × 7 = 455	87 × 3 = 261	49 × 6 = 294	23 × 9 = 207	86 × 4 = 344
5.	35 × 8 = 280	82 × 5 = 410	32 × 9 = 288	46 × 6 = 276	89 × 2 = 178

Page 67 — Check What You Learned: Multiplying 2 Digits by 1 Digit

	a	b	c	d	e
1.	76 × 4 = 304	23 × 6 = 138	57 × 6 = 342	48 × 8 = 384	73 × 9 = 657
2.	49 × 8 = 392	64 × 5 = 320	87 × 9 = 783	43 × 7 = 301	88 × 3 = 264
3.	73 × 6 = 438	54 × 8 = 432	69 × 5 = 345	74 × 9 = 666	39 × 7 = 273
4.	83 × 9 = 747	45 × 6 = 270	75 × 8 = 600	62 × 7 = 434	28 × 9 = 252
5.	52 × 8 = 416	63 × 5 = 315	77 × 3 = 231	38 × 9 = 342	97 × 2 = 194
6.	48 × 7 = 336	53 × 9 = 477	29 × 7 = 203	37 × 8 = 296	82 × 7 = 574

Page 68 — Check What You Know: Problem Solving: Multiplying 2 Digits by 1 Digit

1. 115 cents
2. 295 cents
3. 138 cents
4. 178 cents

Page 69 — Multiplying 2 Digits by 1 Digit

1. $84
2. $168
3. $255

Page 70 — Multiplying 2 Digits by 1 Digit

1. 96 miles
2. 69 miles
3. Roger biked 64 miles. Aaron biked 46 miles.

71

NAME _____ SCORE ⬤ / 3

Multiplying 2 Digits by 1 Digit (with renaming)

Read the problem carefully and solve. Show your work under each question.

Carrie works for a catering company that sells large food platters. The chart on the right shows how many people each platter can feed.

Platter	Number of Meals
Sandwich	28
Salad	37
Pasta	46

Helpful Hint

Rename the top number in a multiplication problem if needed.

Example:
$$\begin{array}{r} \overset{1}{2\,6} \\ \times\ \ 3 \\ \hline 7\,8 \end{array}$$

1. The local bank orders 2 sandwich platters. How many people can these platters feed?

   ___56___ people

2. The convention center orders 3 pasta platters. How many people can these platters feed?

   ___138___ people

3. The teachers at the elementary school order 4 salad platters. How many people can these platters feed?

   ___148___ people

Spectrum Multiplication
Grade 3
Problem Solving: Multiplying 2 Digits by 1 Digit
Chapter 4
71

72

NAME _____ SCORE ⬤ / 3

Multiplication Practice

Read the problem carefully and solve. Show your work under each question.

Asa, Juan, and Suzie are students at the elementary school. They help Ms. Hardy, the school librarian, in the library.

1. The 3 students each take 19 books from the book return and put them back on the shelves. How many books altogether did they put back on the shelves?

   ___57___ books

2. Ms. Hardy asks Juan to put this month's new books on display. There are 6 stacks of new books that Ms. Hardy wants to put on display. There are 28 books in each stack. How many new books are there?

   168

   _____ new books

3. Suzie is going to move 4 shelves of mystery books and 5 shelves of fiction books to a different part of the library. There are 32 books on each shelf. How many books will Suzie move?

   _____ books

Spectrum Multiplication
Grade 3
Problem Solving: Multiplying 2 Digits by 1 Digit
Chapter 4
72

73

NAME _____ SCORE ⬤ / 3

Multiplication Practice

Solve each problem. Show your work under each question.

1. There are 40 chicken farms near an Ohio town. If each farm has 9 barns, how many total barns are there?

   360

   There are _____ total barns.

2. Mr. Ferris has a canoe rental business. Over the weekend, he rented 47 canoes. A canoe holds 3 people. If each canoe was full, how many people did Mr. Ferris rent to over the weekend?

   Mr. Ferris rented to _____ people.
   368

3. The school planned for 92 students to attend the school dance. The school bought 4 slices of pizza for each student. How many slices did the school buy?

   The school bought _____ slices.

Spectrum Multiplication
Grade 3
Problem Solving: Multiplying 2 Digits by 1 Digit
Chapter 4
73

74

NAME _____ SCORE ⬤ / 3

Multiplication Practice

Solve each problem. Show your work under each question.

1. The pool opened on Memorial Day. Ninety-four people showed up. The pool manager gave out 2 vouchers to each person for free drinks. How many vouchers did the pool manager give out?

   188

   The manager gave out _____ vouchers.

2. In the Sumton community, there are 56 houses. If there are 3 children living in each house, how many children live in houses in Sumton?
   168

   There are _____ children living in houses in Sumton.
   115

3. Deon and Denise are saving up to buy a computer game. If they put 23 dollars a week in the bank, how much money will they have in 5 weeks?

   They will have _____ dollars.

Spectrum Multiplication
Grade 3
Problem Solving: Multiplying 2 Digits by 1 Digit
Chapter 4
74

75

NAME _____ SCORE ⬤ / 3

Multiplication Practice

Solve each problem. Show your work under each question.

1. Xavier loves to eat pears. He ate 2 a day for 48 days. How many pears did Xavier eat?

   96

   Xavier ate _____ pears.

2. Clayton keeps pet mice. If his 33 mice have 4 babies each, how many mice will Clayton have in all?
   132

   Clayton will have _____ mice.
   275

3. A class of 55 students went on a field trip to collect seashells. If the students collected 5 shells each, how many shells did they collect?

   The students collected _____ shells.

Spectrum Multiplication
Grade 3
Problem Solving: Multiplying 2 Digits by 1 Digit
Chapter 4
75

76

NAME _____ SCORE ⬤ / 3

Multiplication Practice

Solve each problem. Show your work under each question.

1. John bought four 23-cent stamps. How many cents did John spend on stamps?

   The stamps cost ___92___ cents.

2. A clown had 13 balloons that he sold at a carnival for 5 cents each. If he sold all 13 balloons, how much money did he make?

   The clown made ___65___ cents.

3. The movie rental store charges 3 dollars to rent each movie. Miss Padilla rents 5 movies. How much will the movie rental store charge her?

   The movie rental store will charge Miss Padilla ___15___ dollars.

Spectrum Multiplication
Grade 3
Problem Solving: Multiplying 2 Digits by 1 Digit
Chapter 4
76

Spectrum Multiplication
Grade 3

Answer Key

Answer Key

Page 77

Check What You Learned
Problem Solving: Multiplying 2 Digits by 1 Digit

Read the problem carefully and solve. Show your work under each question.

Erin is having a yard sale. She is selling books for $3, toys for $5, and dishes for $2.

1. Lee buys 14 toys. How much does this cost?
$70

2. Erin's teacher, Mr. Garcia, buys 8 animal books and 16 fiction books for his classroom. How much does this cost?
$72

3. Ms. Kwan lives next door to Erin. She buys 23 dishes at the yard sale. How much does this cost?
$46

4. Kim works at the youth center. She buys 17 toys at the yard sale. How much does this cost?
$85

Spectrum Multiplication Grade 3 — Chapter 4 — Problem Solving: Multiplying 2 Digits by 1 Digit — 77

Page 78

Final Test Chapters 1–4

Multiply.

	a	b	c	d	e
1.	13 ×5 = 65	7 ×2 = 14	10 ×0 = 0	81 ×4 = 324	42 ×2 = 84
2.	52 ×3 = 156	76 ×5 = 380	41 ×5 = 205	3 ×2 = 6	14 ×3 = 42
3.	45 ×5 = 225	93 ×3 = 279	42 ×3 = 126	33 ×2 = 66	10 ×5 = 50
4.	51 ×2 = 102	91 ×1 = 91	17 ×5 = 85	31 ×2 = 62	25 ×5 = 125
5.	32 ×5 = 160	8 ×7 = 56	5 ×9 = 45	4 ×0 = 0	38 ×1 = 38
6.	6 ×9 = 54	4 ×7 = 28	22 ×1 = 22	19 ×3 = 57	83 ×2 = 166
7.	6 ×5 = 30	53 ×3 = 159	18 ×4 = 72	8 ×6 = 48	13 ×2 = 26
8.	7 ×4 = 28	5 ×0 = 0	3 ×2 = 6	8 ×2 = 16	56 ×2 = 112

Spectrum Multiplication Grade 3 — Final Test Chapters 1–4 — 78

Page 79

Final Test Chapters 1–4

Multiply.

	a	b	c	d	e
9.	1 ×5 = 5	9 ×9 = 81	3 ×2 = 6	5 ×4 = 20	6 ×3 = 18
10.	9 ×7 = 63	5 ×2 = 10	6 ×1 = 6	8 ×2 = 16	5 ×7 = 35
11.	6 ×5 = 30	8 ×3 = 24	4 ×3 = 12	0 ×8 = 0	6 ×2 = 12
12.	13 ×2 = 26	23 ×4 = 92	17 ×5 = 85	42 ×1 = 42	18 ×0 = 0
13.	54 ×2 = 108	96 ×2 = 192	53 ×3 = 159	33 ×2 = 66	11 ×5 = 55

Complete each table.

14.
a. Rule: multiply by 4

In	Out
1	4
5	20
7	28
8	32

b. Rule: multiply by 8

In	Out
3	24
6	48
4	32
8	64

c. Rule: multiply by 7

In	Out
4	28
0	0
7	49
1	7

Spectrum Multiplication Grade 3 — Final Test Chapters 1–4 — 79

Page 80

Final Test Chapters 1–4

Multiply.

	a	b	c	d	e
15.	2 ×0 = 0	5 ×1 = 5	4 ×3 = 12	0 ×2 = 0	5 ×6 = 30
16.	7 ×2 = 14	9 ×3 = 27	8 ×8 = 64	6 ×3 = 18	4 ×5 = 20
17.	6 ×6 = 36	3 ×9 = 27	1 ×7 = 7	5 ×3 = 15	2 ×6 = 12
18.	3 ×0 = 0	4 ×7 = 28	6 ×9 = 54	4 ×4 = 16	5 ×1 = 5
19.	7 ×4 = 28	3 ×7 = 21	2 ×3 = 6	4 ×2 = 8	9 ×1 = 9
20.	20 ×4 = 80	14 ×3 = 42	29 ×3 = 87	32 ×4 = 128	96 ×2 = 192
21.	46 ×4 = 184	72 ×1 = 72	61 ×3 = 183	70 ×2 = 140	52 ×4 = 208
22.	21 ×5 = 105	15 ×3 = 45	31 ×4 = 124	90 ×2 = 180	56 ×3 = 168

Spectrum Multiplication Grade 3 — Final Test Chapters 1–4 — 80

Page 81

Final Test Chapters 1–4

Solve each problem.

23. Kiri has 15 apples to share equally with 5 friends. Write a multiplication equation to find how many apples Kiri gave to each friend. Then, solve.
5 x a = 15   3 apples.

24. Each of Mr. Black's 4 daughters needs new shoes. Each pair of shoes will cost 29 dollars. How much money will Mr. Black spend on all 4 pairs of shoes?
Mr. Black will spend 116 dollars on the 4 pairs of shoes.

25. There are 30 students in each classroom. If there are 5 classrooms, how many total students are there?
There are a total of 150 students.

26. There are 7 friends that each have 2 dollars. How much money do the 7 friends have?
The friends have a total of 14 dollars.

27. Write the rule for this table.

In	Out
4	16
6	24
8	32
9	36

multiply by 4

Spectrum Multiplication Grade 3 — Final Test Chapters 1–4 — 81

Page 82

Final Test Chapters 1–4

Solve each problem. Show your work under each question.

28. Gary read 3 books with 56 pages each. How many pages did he read in all?
There are 56 pages in each book.
Gary read 3 books.
Gary read 168 pages in all.

29. There are 5 classes at a school. Each class has 32 students. How many students are at the school?
There are 32 students in each class.
There are 5 classes.
There are 160 students in the school.

30. Yolanda bought 4 boxes of cookies for a party. If each box has 24 cookies, how many cookies does she have in all?
Each box has 24 cookies.
Yolanda bought 4 boxes of cookies.
Yolanda bought a total of 96 cookies.

31. During a football game, 2 teams play against each other. There are 11 football players on the field for each team. How many football players are on the field during a football game?
There are 22 football players on the field.

Spectrum Multiplication Grade 3 — Final Test Chapters 1–4 — 82